EMBRACING EPIPHANY MOMENT

I0150615

Ajit Nair

Become
Shakespeare
.com

First published in 2018 by
Becomeshakespeare.com
Wordit Content Design & Editing Services Pvt Ltd
Unit - 26, Building A-1, Nr Wadala RTO, Wadala (East),
Mumbai 400037, India
T:+91 8080226699

This book has been funded by WORDIT ART FUND
WORDIT ART FUND helps deserving
Authors publish their work
To apply for funding, please visit us at
becomeshakespeare.com

©
ISBN: 978-93-87649-17-0

Disclaimer:
This is a work of fiction. Names, characters, business,
place, event and incidents are either the product of the
author's imagination or used in a fictitious manner. Any
resemblance to actual person, living or dead or actual
event is purely coincidental.

ACKNOWLEDGEMENT

With Humble Gratitute to Matha, Pitha,
Guru, Daivom

With Love To *Mahatria*

CONTENTS

PROLOGUE

The daily work schedule and weekends with family left me with little time to read and write. In order to make the best of this limited time, I thought of scripting some short stories that are interesting and do not take much of time to read. The results of this exercise are being presented herewith as a bouquet of myriad short-stories.

Every person has an interesting story to tell. During the tenure of my service, I have met several persons and some of them had fascinating stories to tell derived from their real life experiences. Such stories have been picked up and the thoughts evolved and expressed in words, with an intent to reinforce positivism at the end of each story. I have tried to recreate those events, places and conversations from my memories of them. In order to maintain their anonymity in some instances, I have changed the names of individuals and places. In some cases, I have also changed certain identifiable characteristics and details such as physical properties, occupations and places of residence.

The realization that life is simple and we can keep it the same way with just two basic principles of (a) stop expecting from others and (b) start accepting the things the way it is, has made life beautiful and worth living in the present. My stories evolve from these thoughts and hence, this book is called "EMBRACING EPIPHANY MOMENT", as we have different expressions of emotional reaction to every situation. If these reactions are understood in true spirit as experiences given by GOD with a revelation and the energy is channelized properly towards a larger good, the world can become a beautiful place to live together.

This book is an innocent attempt with a singular purpose of motivating the reader. Hence, if any reader does not like or agree with the contents herein, I proffer my humble apologies for the same in advance in the benefit of larger interest.

I dedicate this book to all those who inspired me by touching my life at some point of time through their teachings and experiences. My special thanks and gratitude to my loving guru, Mahatria from Infinitheism who showed me the path of life and taught me to live life with peace and happiness, thereby making the optimum good of this valuable gift we all have received. My Guru, this book is by you through me. My humble gratitude and love to my parents - this is from you. My loving wife Aruna and my adorable son Abhishek, this is for you.

My sincere thanks to the publishing house, Becomeshakespeare.com who saw value in this book and hence have invested their valuable time and resource in bringing this book to you.

I would like to thank my Mentors Mr. KK Menon, Mr. Vikas Gupta, Dr. Rajesh Jain, Mr. Masood Alam, Dr. Yash Goyal, Mr. Radhakrishnan Menon who have influenced me and touched my life positively. Thanking my friends Jagdish Nair and Sudhir Nair who have been supportive and have accepted me as what i am.

My humble thanks with gratitude to all the readers of this book. God bless all with abundance of humbleness, peace, happiness and devotion. Look forward to that EPIPHANY moment in your life and make the best of it. GOD BLESS YOU!!!

Chapter 1

You Can Hate Me !!!!

A ravind and Asha, both students of MBA studying in Pune in the same class. They had a fondness for each other, as they shared a common liking for scriptures and discussions on various aspects of humanity, philosophies and spiritualism. This closeness led them to a relationship where both nurtured exceptional love for each other. Their love had no boundaries and they expressed an immaculate affection and care for each other. Their friends envied their togetherness and hoped to find a companion like that for themselves. Few of their friends, out of mere jealousy felt, this was all a show-off!!

However, only time would tell the reality!!!!

Aravind, a native of Kerala was planning a vacation with his cousins and checked if Asha would be comfortable joining him. He had planned to drive down in his new car – a gift from his father. The drive would be a long thrilling journey all the way from Pune to Trivandrum. More than the thrill, Asha was interested in Aravind's company and hence willingly accepted to join him.

Both started on a Saturday morning from the Pune expressway. The drive was indeed thrilling and exciting. The duo kept chattering incessantly, getting to know each other more deeply by exchanging their thoughts and sharing their experiences of childhood days, their friends and so on. The fields on both sides of the road were lush green and the crops were dancing with the serene breeze. Asha's face resembled an energizing nectar, ready to flow, glowing with the sunrays that pierced through the branches on the sides of the road as the vehicle sped fast towards its destination. Aravind was in a state of thrall, driving as he was with his love on his side and captivated by the beautiful surroundings through which they were passing.

And then alas!!!.... just over a mountain climb, Aravind lost control of the steering-wheel due to huge truck that speedily overtook their car, throwing the vehicle into a valley deep down 100 ft. The massive accident turned the car into a lump of steel. Aravind and Asha were stuck badly inside the car, struggling for their life. The villagers from near-by village who heard the sound of the car hurtling down the valley, rushed to the site. Seeing two lives struggling to hold on, the villagers felt a pull of humanity. They removed them from the car and rushed them to the near-by hospital.

Asha was critical and unconscious and had severe injuries to her left side of the body. She was unconscious for nearly three days. When she regained consciousness, she was still incoherent and struggling to recollect what happened. Soon, the doctor came to her room and in soothing, concerned tone, conveyed the unfortunate news saying "My child, the impact of accident was terrible, but thank God that you are alive. However, you have unfortunately lost your eye sight. You need to be strong to accept this reality. You had serious damages to your entire left hand and so we had to amputate it. Even your face has some burn marks, which cannot be treated now. They shall be treated by surgery once you cope up with your present condition".

The Doctors words shattered Asha. She tried to feel her left hand which was no more there; she tried touching her face with her right hand to feel the scars, but the nurse warned her not to do so. It took her a couple of days to reconcile with this dreadful situation. Being an inherently positive-minded person, she decided to focus on regaining her confidence and live life afresh from now without looking back. However, her mind was also curious about Aravind, who hadn't come to see her for the past few days. She wondered, why? Asha's mind started conjuring dreadful thoughts about Aravind; she tried to quell them but it was difficult. Asha's parents and her best friend Anusha were all along with her in the hospital and that was the only moral support she had at this time of distress.

As the treatment progressed, one thing which kept Asha's mind occupied was, why did all this have to happen to me and why Aravind is not with me? After a few more agonizing days, Asha garnered courage and asked Anusha to enquire about Aravind. Later that day, Anusha returned with some good news for Asha. "Asha, by God's grace Aravind is fine and recovering fast. He should be discharged from the hospital any day now". This gave Asha some relief.

On the other side, Asha's parents started getting extremely worried about her future. They were mainly concerned about how she could get out of this mental trauma and what treatment would best suit her.

Doctors attempt to counsel Asha's parents by explaining that the burn marks on Asha's face were comparatively minor and could be overcome with plastic surgery. They also gave them hope saying Asha's eyesight could also be restored if they got a suitable retina-donor. However, the doctors also cautioned them that "we do not recommend any solution for the left arm as of now, because in the condition that she is in right now, it will be difficult for Asha to adjust to an artificial limb."

Within the next two days, the ophthalmologist came in with some great news for Asha. They had found a suitable retina-donor for her and hence, Asha could see again. Soon, Asha's eyes were operated upon; alongside, she also had the plastic surgery performed. Within a month, Asha was again bubbling with life with her eye-sight back to normal and the hope of a beautiful face rejuvenated in her heart. Now her new rays of eyes started looking out for Aravind all the time, but in vain.

One day, just before Asha is about to get discharged from the hospital, Sukumar, Aravind's cousin drops in to meet her. He introduces himself to Asha and inquires about her health. Asha is keen to hear about Aravind, but Sukumar is reluctant to speak a word. Finally, after a long time, he hands over a letter to Asha stating "Asha, this letter is for you from Aravind. Please read it carefully. Bye." Saying this, Sukumar leaves the hospital.

Asha struggles with one hand to open the envelope, pulls the paper out and holds the letter to read. "Asha, my love, sorry to know what has happened to you. I understand it's my mistake. But life must go on. You are free to live your life the way you want and I am free the way I want. Let's not cross each other's path. Take care."

The letter slips out of Asha's fingers, just as tears start pouring from her eyes. Her sorrow knows no boundaries; she feels as if the whole world has collapsed on her. The sense that she has been dumped by Aravind makes her feel miserable. Shattered by what has happened, she suddenly feels lost. She starts feeling as if there are no answers to her own life; as if, her life has become one meaningless void with no one to care for.

However, being a strong personality, Asha gets over this shock in due course. She decides to live for her parents and live to prove that she cannot be ignored and treated like this!!! She decides to appear for the IAS entrance exam. Her sharp wit and hard-work help Asha achieve the top position in that extremely difficult competitive exam and from thereon, Asha never looks back! She proves her mettle by becoming the best IAS officer and dedicates her life to the social cause and upliftment of the backward class. She ensures that justice prevails for all and its execution is done with full integrity. Naturally, name, fame and honor all follow her.

After serving for nearly 20 years in various parts of the country, Asha gets transferred to a small village named Neyyatingara near Trivandrum in Kerala. Situated on the way to Kanyakumari, this village is an important business zone. Hence, a need was felt to develop the village and help uplift the villagers; and who better than Asha to take up this work? Thus it was that Asha got posted over there.

The village was small but it loomed large on Asha's mind, because the name of the village opened up a treasure-trove of Aravind related memories for her. Initially, it got difficult for her to control the wave of nostalgia that swept over her. But soon, true to her personality, Asha reined in her emotions and took charge of her new assignment.

Few months passed by. Asha was getting into the thick of the activities in her Village Government office at Neyyatingara. One day, while arbitrating a land dispute matter, she came across Sukumar who was pleading for original ownership of the disputed land. Sukumar immediately recalled Asha and was thrilled to see her as well as her success.

Asha, however, was washed over by a wave of bitterness seeing Sukumar, but she determinedly maintained her calm. Sukumar, keenly observing her expressions realized her emotions and hence decided to stay back and talk to Asha alone, later.

Once the official matters was discussed and recorded, every one left the room, except Sukumar who waited back to have talk with Asha. When Sukumar, in a formal way, inquired about her, Asha steadfastly refused to discuss her personal life with him. However, she was also growing curious to know how was Aravind, and with that, she also wanted to make him realize what she has gained over the years due to her dedication. Sukumar kept inquiring politely about Asha's life but refused to say anything about Aravind. Asha also did not ask anything initially.

Then, her patience ran out and she directly asked Sukumar, "How is Aravind? Where he is these days?"

Hearing her question, Sukumar politely invited her to his house saying, "I can fix up a direct meeting with him and you may get all your answers directly from him tomorrow itself. Asha was stun-shocked to realize that Aravind was very much in the same village and she was getting a chance to meet him. That night, she could barely sleep; mixed emotions about meeting Aravind playing truant with her mind. She was keen to meet him, to see how life had turned out for him; but all the same, she was also aware that she was a different person today than she was that time. So also must it be with Aravind.

He must be having his own family and what gave her the right to interfere in their affairs? After much tossing & turning, Asha decides that she will visit Aravind for a few minutes and promptly return.

The next day turns out to be a very tough one for Asha. Every minute seems like an hour and she feels as if she has never waited for anything so long in life. At last, with the sun lowering its rays, the working day coming to an end. Asha returns home, changes into her best outfit, and applies elegant make-up. Then, she travels towards Sukumar's given address with her heartbeat increasing with every turn of the wheel. Finally, she reaches the gates of Sukumar's home where she would be meeting Aravind in a couple of minutes.

Asha is warmly welcomed by Sukumar and his family and offered some snacks and tea. After a short chat with Sukumar, she enquires about Aravind and his family. Sukumar hesitatingly walks inside the house and returns with a book and hands it over to Asha. Asha glances through the book which has all her photographs and the letters written by her to Aravind and at the end, there is a sealed envelope.

Asha looks at Sukumar with a puzzled expression. Sukumar asks her to open that envelope as he do not know what Aravind has written for her. She hurriedly unseals the envelope and starts tearing through the words in a hurry!

"My love Asha, I never wanted to be your weakness and the truth was something which you wouldn't have accepted. Hence I had to create a hate for me in you so that you would challenge yourself to succeed. That, I thought, was the only way I could create a purpose for you in your life. I am sure you may come searching for me one day, but by then you must have settled well in life and must be highly respected in what you must be doing then. I only want to support you in that mission. I am writing this letter today with great difficulty. These are probably the last few days of mine. But I shall always be alive within you and shall see this whole world through you through my eyes which I am bestowing to you."

Asha's hands start trembling and tears start rolling down her eyes - rather Aravind's eyes! Unknown to her, she had been seeing the world for last two decades with her beloved Aravind's eyes! She is deeply stirred by Aravind's sacrifice and feels a swell of pride for his selfless love. With grief of having lost Aravind and the pride of keeping him alive within her, she silently walks out of Sukumar's house.

Asha doesn't report to work for the next few days. Soon after, she requests for a transfer to her home town and leaves the village. Sukumar feels worried about whether Aravind's sacrifice is going to be in vain. Whether Aravind's gesture has been so large in magnitude that it has shaken Asha that she has been unable to withstand the deep emotions beneath it.

Few years pass by. One day, as Sukumar sits watching a news-channel, he comes across editorial special feature on 'ordinary persons with extra-ordinary contributions'. Sukumar's eyes fill up with tears as he sees the coverage regarding a NGO for Disabled persons run successfully by a well-educated Government official. This NGO is operated with a personal touch and care, making it unique and different than all other organisations. That organization was called "Aravindashram" and was run by none other than Asha !!!

A humble beginning for a mega purpose of serving humanity!!!

~~~ ~~~ ~~~

Chapter 2

Fight for Justice

Shriman Shirish Thakur is a young educated collector in the Government service who stands for truth, justice and equality. He was transferred thrice in his short duration of service for standing by these values and possessing a strong character. However, this did not discourage Shirish and he continued to serve with complete focus on his ingrained values. He was well-known for his justice towards the locals and his empathy for the suppressed class and that's why he was also called "Garibon ka rakshak"(Saviour of the Poor).

As his transfers continued due to political influencing, Shirish gets transferred to Mapusa district. On moving into his new office, he immediately rolls up his sleeves to understand the city administration, villages nearby, the key decision makers, etc.

Ghadchincholi, a small village on the outskirts of the city was one name that kept being repeatedly discussed in his presence and Shirish was curious to know more about what was so interesting about this place. He decided to call for a small meeting of his direct reportees, the office bearers, to understand the matters concerning Ghadchincholi.

The discussion was to understand the pending files and matters related to this small village. From the discussion, Shirish gathered that it was a small village, strategically located on the way of a major Express Highway project and once the highway project commenced, it would be an ideal site for a posh shopping mall, food plaza and fuel refilling center. The land mafia was obviously having a vulture's eye on this land to make some seriously big money. Shirish also understands that all the files with the department are of the land registration papers from those persons who have purchased the land from the villagers and now want to consolidate these pieces into a single land for the mega project. Shirish is not clear with the discussion and hence insists on inspecting the land personally. The office bearers, instead, provide him with the photographs of the land which clarifies to Shirish that it is just a plain barren land with sparse growth of wild bushes across and that there is no activity on that land. He is now lead to the point of conviction that the process of barren land consolidation and registration for commercial gain occurring due to an upcoming project should not be a concern. But his inner consciousness keeps forcing him to hold back his decision. He insists a thorough study of the file before giving his sanction.

Few days pass by and Shirish remains busy in his daily affairs. He normally spends his weekends at home relaxing, reading newspapers or clearing official files. On one such Sunday evening, in a very relaxed mood, Shirish is enjoying the nature's beauty with his left arm resting on the window pane and the right hand holding a mug of coffee, which he is sipping in between, enjoying the chirping of birds and revelling in the dark clouds passing by. He can smell the mud, and guesses that it is about to rain. Deciding to enjoy the sight of the rain, Shirish continues to linger at the window. Soon, a few droplets start touching the ground, leading to a beautiful sheet of white rain pouring down soon after. Shirish gets drawn into the beauty of the drops of life that God has created through rains. He decides to take a walk in the rain and get himself drenched.

He moves out of his house, walking through an isolated street with nature's beauty at its peak flourishing all around. Along the way, Shirish's attention gets suddenly diverted to a group of around ten to twelve villagers standing on the side of the street, completely soaked and shivering in the rains with no shelter to protect them. He notices that their clothes are torn, they have no footwear and even the rains couldn't hide the tears in their eyes. They keep looking at Shirish as if they have something to express to him and Shirish's steps get drawn towards them as if by some magnetic pull. As Shirish goes closer, they fall on his feet crying "Babu, you are the only savior for us. Save our land".

Shirish gets perplexed and is unable to comprehend the situation. He invites all of them to his house and makes them seated comfortably in the veranda. Then, he asks them to explain in detail what they expect from him. The villagers sit on the floor at the corner side of the veranda, still hesitant of making an eye to eye contact with their savior. Shirish offers them tea, but they politely refuse saying they would not dream of taking anything from their benefactor.

Shirish then inquires about their whereabouts. One of the villager starts telling in broken local language: "Sir, we are farmers from Ghadchincholi and our community have been staying there for the past ten decades". Shirish now connects the reason for their visit and goads them for further details to facilitate taking an informative decision on this matter.

Thus the conversation commences:

Shirish : But I understand it's a barren land and it has been so for years now.

Villager : Sir, those are all fictitious records. We and all our earlier generations have stayed in that place. It was our great grandfathers who came first and settled in this place when there was nothing. Their hard work and dedication got that land converted to a good farming ground. They used to grow tamarind trees and also cultivate few other vegetables. That sacred place also had a small fort with a goddess temple. Hence, it was called as "Ghad" for the fort and "Chinch" for its tamarind. Few families settled at that place. With progress in cultivation, few more families joined. Later a panchayat was formed in Ghadchincholi. Slowly we had a paathshala (pre-school) for children's education and a small market to barter the cultivation.

Shirish : What do you expect from me?

Villagers : Babu, now the land mafia is after our land. We had a peaceful life till now. However, now it's a life of threat and terror!!! Our kids and ladies do not feel safe. The greed for money has made these hooligans cross all boundaries of harassment while dealing with their fellow brothers and sisters!!! Their sole aim is to vacate us from this land by hook or crook. That land is our mother and no one can separate us from our mother!!!

Shirish : The matter seems complicated, as all records show it's a barren land.

Villagers : Babu, should you insist to have a personal inspection, one of us can accompany you in your vehicle and take you to Ghadchincholi. You should visit the place and see for yourself for conviction and your personal conscience. We shall not interfere in the decision that you shall take after that. However, we insist that you should visit us alone and not be accompanied with your officers or any of the land mafia person. Please trust us. We have only you to look upto.

Shirish : If that is so, let me visit the place tomorrow itself.

The villagers bless Shirish with teary eyes and leave, retaining behind one of the villagers to escort Shirish to the village next day. The villager sleeps outside Shirish's house that night.

Next day, Shirish starts early in the morning towards Ghadchincholi along with the villager in his car. Shirish decides to drive himself to ensure that even the driver is not with him. On the way, the villager narrates various stories about the village and their association to that place. Shirish observes that all the incidences narrated by that villager are of good memories, love, peace, harmony and respect only, positively reinforcing their attachment to that place. By afternoon, they reach the village. Shirish is stunned to see a beautiful marvel in front of him, a village which is blessed by the Mother Nature.

Shirish is welcomed by the same set of eleven villagers whom he had met the previous evening. He runs his eyes around to gather what all he can capture in his memory. Shirish sees a banyan tree with a sit-out, a well where few ladies are washing their clothes, a paathshala for children with a capacity of around a dozen children, a bullock cart, few huts made of mud walls and topped up by hay for shelter, a small play-ground and behind all these, a beautiful field where various kinds of vegetables are being grown. Shirish knows that all these couldn't be built overnight and most of these looked very old. Hence, he draws a conclusion that this place is in existence for long and the villagers' claim is true. The Sarpanch of the village is introduced to Shirish and he insists that Shirish should have lunch in his hut along with other villagers. Shirish finds this offer polite and humane and visits the Sarpanch's house. All men sit together for a simple meal of hot rotis and potato curry. The serving is done with love and compassion. By now, Shirish gets to know a few of the villagers by name. He inspects the village thoroughly and observes that all the people are looking at him with eyes shining with expectation that Shirish will do something to help them. During the conversation with the Sarpanch, Shirish gathers that few kilometers away there is another village named Ratlampur which is an extended arm of this village and both these villages share a good relation in trade, culture and marriages.

The sarpanch of Ratlampur is Ganpat Shinde and he is a great supporter of this village.

Soon, dusk falls and Shirish realizes its time for him to return. He thanks the villagers and leaves the village. While driving back, his mind is filled with many unanswered questions about the files that are placed in his office.

Next morning, Shirish decides to scan through the files again before calling for a discussion. After reading through the file and getting convinced that the claim in the file is about a barren land, Shirish calls for a meeting with the office bearers and the concerned land mafia members whose files have been put forth for registration. The meeting is scheduled in two day's time. Shirish still remains in a dilemma of such a gross mistake in reality and records !!!

The meeting starts on the scheduled day at the scheduled time with six of his office bearers and eight investors in that land. Shirish steers the meeting with the question "Is the claim about the land genuine?" Half of the team in the room look at each other baffled and attempt to understand the question. A few also have a look of guilt on their face and are unable to meet Shirish's eye. Rounds of justification increase the temperature of that room as few office bearers are silent on the issue; few of them supporting Shirish; and the investors rationalizing their claim, reasoning for their right on that property and the need for the same to be registered in their favor as a pooled land. Shirish then releases the cat out of the box. He communicates that few days back he had been to Ghadchincholi and has seen a well-established village with people, children, paathshala, well, panchayat and farm lands. He also shares his experience of having lunch with them. The room is suddenly filled with silence. Even the wind gushing through the room can be heard – such is the pindrop silence that ensues!!!

After a few minutes pass by in such silence, one investor gets up with an attempt to shatter the latest revelation made by Shirish.

Investor : Saheb, with due respect, what's there to see where there is just dust and acres of barren land?

Shirish : Its an utter non-truth as I have personally visited the place.

One of the office bearer : Saheb, you may be wrong or must have seen some other place, as I have inspected this place just 4 months back and have reported that in the file as well. There is no village on that land as you are describing.

Other investor, now gaining confidence : Someone must have mislead you and there is no need to get emotional. You have seen the photos. Please don't waste any more time. Just clear the proposal Shirish Saheb!!!

The debate continues for some time, but now its Shirish on one side and the entire team on the other. As the discussion prolongs, unknowingly a passing statement by an office bearer pulls Shirish's attention.

An Office bearer : Saheb must have dreamt all about this incidence and is now trying to justify it to us! Otherwise how can you ever see a village established over a grave yard!!!

This was the second shocker of the day and it was too much now for Shirish to handle. He insisted for more details, but realizing his mistake, the office bearer pretends having said nothing. Few investors decide to move out of the meeting on the pretext of some urgent work. The meeting gets called off abruptly with no resolution.

Shirish is deeply perturbed and immediately starts for Ghadchincholi along with two of his trusted office bearers. As his vehicle moves on, he observes a car following him. His colleague tells Shirish that the car belongs to one of the investors who had walked out of the meeting. This does not bother Shirish, as his heart is now only beating to know what the state of that village is.

The inspection team reaches Ghadchincholi by evening and in a state of shock, Shirish moves out of the car with his eyes trying to run around and see if he can find anything resembling what he had witnessed few days back. Alas, he cannot see anything around. All around, he only sees a charred land with dust accumulated all over it. In a state of despair, Shirish runs into that charred land filled with black dust all around and no traces of life!!! It becomes clear to him that there has been no trace of life on this land for many years now! Shirish helplessly falls to his knees, his eyes brimming with tears about not understanding what this is all about. His office bearers now approach Shirish and gently pat him on the back. Shirish controls his emotions and gets up. Now he looks around in search of details and observes that in place of the paathshala, now stood a broken wall structure and where he had seen the well, a deep hollow structure existed.

Shirish is now convinced that there is something different to this episode and wants to get to the root of it. Suddenly he is reminded of Ratlampur and its Sarpanch Ganesh Shinde, who one of the villagers had mentioned in passing during their 'conversation'. Shirish insists on going to Ratlampur. His office bearers empathize with their Saheb and wish to join him. As they proceed, they notice the car that was following them is returning back, maybe convinced that the inspection is complete to their satisfaction!!!

The team of three reaches Ratlampur by late evening. They inquire about the Sarpanch Ganesh

Shinde. With great respect, they are taken to Ganesh's house. Shirish observes that the houses at Ratlampur are similar to what he saw in Ghadchincholi and even the culture and lifestyle of the people seemed similar. At the Sarpanch's house, they are asked to be seated on a well-scrubbed floor. A single bulb provides illumination to the small but neat room. Soon, Ganesh Shinde appears in front of Shirish and his team. They are welcomed with cool butter milk and as Ganesh sits down in front of them, he inquires about the reason for their visit. Shirish introduces himself and his team members to the Sarpanch and with a bit of hesitation and eagerness shares the purpose of his visit.

Shirish : Sarpanchji, I have come to you with a great dilemma in front of me. I am the collector of this district and am handling the case of land registrations of Ghadchincholi. Last week I was approached by a few villagers of Ghadchincholi who pleaded to me that as they stay there, no privatization of that land should be done in favor of land mafia and investors. I also personally visited the place and met the villagers. Based on this, when I tried to protect their interest, I was told that nothing exists in Ghadchincholi and hence today I came again for an inspection. To my utter shock, I found nothing there except charred land, as if no

life had existed over it for years now. I am
completely mystified. The only thing I could
remember was your name as told to me by the
Sarpanch whom I met during my visit of that
village, which today no more exists!!! I have
come to you to see if you can help me understand
the reality and solve this puzzle for me.

As Shirish was narrating this, he could see Ganesh's
face clouding with emotions, eyes turning wet and the
pearls of tears rolling down and accumulating over his
mustache. Ganesh was without words for some time
and sat covering his face with his palms for a long
time. Shirish could sense the gravity of the situation,
but was also getting impatient. He gets up and walks
towards Ganesh and touches his head with respect as
if telling him to look at Shirish. Ganesh gets over his
emotional outburst and looks straight into Shirish's
eyes . Everyone around is waiting with bated breath to
hear what Ganesh Shinde has to say:

Ganesh : Ghadchincholi was a lovely village, rich in
culture and respect for humanity. We at
Ratlampur have imbibed their life style so that
we can also be a happy village. Ghadchincholi
always lived for happiness and prosperity.
Prosperity for them was not money, but
education, progress in cultivation, sports,

building up equality and living for others. They had adopted Bouddh dharma and believed in the teachings of Lord Buddha. We were happy giving our daughters in marriage to that village, as they always treated women with respect. We were also happy marrying our boys to the girls from that village as they brought in their rich culture into our village, a culture of peace, harmony, love and respect. However, all good things had to end for Ghadchincholi. The Express Highway project was announced and Ghadchincholi became the focal point for some greedy money makers who had no humanity left in them. They approached the villagers and offered money to vacate the land and sell it to them. The villagers did not fall prey to these money as the motive for their life was not materialistic gain but spiritual alignment. The entire village was one united force living with peace and harmony and perceiving every individual as their extended brothers and sisters. Such was the purity of thoughts of those villagers.

But the land mafia did not relent. They tried all means - through pressure, through harassment, though humiliation, through force, through terrorizing, but all in vain. The villagers, united with a peaceful harmony, withstood all these through love and non-violence. They also approached the law and order department and filed complaints against these errant land mafia, pleading for protection, but in vain. Time was now catching up and the land mafia was running short of patience on this land-grabbing deal. Hence they came out with an atrocious plan and executed it one night by setting the entire village ablaze. Everything was burnt out, not a single life was spared, all cultivation was charred. The well became a hoard of dead bodies. All peace, harmony, love and respect was converted to a furnace filled with orange flames of fire!!!

Ganesh, thus continued: Today after hearing from you, I am proud that my friends, even after their death, continue to fight for justice and that too with peace, harmony, love and respect!!!. I am convinced that man is mortal but the values we live with are immortal!!!

Shirish was stunned to hear this story from Ganesh. It felt as if his entire body had become numb. Without uttering a word, Shirish gives a soft squeeze to Ganesh's folded hands and slips out of his house. On the way back, there is complete silence in the car. Shirish's office bearers also have nothing to express after this astonishing revelation.

The night that follows is one of complete disruption for Shirish as all the incidents of last one week keep haunting him. Ganesh's profound words keep reverberating in his mind: "MAN IS MORTAL

BUT THE VALUES WE LIVE WITH, ARE IMMORTAL".

Shirish decides to live for these newly discovered values and dedicate his life for the cause of humanity. He gets determined to walk the path that shall serve humanity and with this aim, approaches few of his friends from who he can expect some funding to start a center for those deprived and re-develop the place called Ghadchincholi.

God never gives us an experience unless there is some learning in it. Shirish's learning of living for others is one such experiential turning point. Also, God gives ideas only to those who can execute it. Hence, as Shirish was the chosen one, the path was laid clear for him. His good intentions made money available for him easily. His plea to the Government to hand over the land of Ghadchincholi under long-term lease for his project of building a self-sustained village for the deprived class, was cleared. Few like-minded people joined Shirish in his deliberation. All Shirish had to do then was to build a model village of Ghadchincholi by relocating few persons deprived of a respectful living and hand-hold them towards a life filled with a culture of education, respect for motherland, love for others, peace, harmony, brotherhood and a life of emotional and spiritual alignment. Shirish spent the rest of his life in Ghadchincholi with happiness as the source of everything.

Chapter 3

Eternal Love

Nirmala is a nurse in the cancer patient's ward of a municipal hospital. She is someone who believes that 'to nurse a patient well, we have to feel their pain and understand them'. With this thought, she spends hours listening to each patient, trying to make them feel utmost comfortable. Through this gesture, Nirmala not only provides physical care but also, much-needed emotional succour to help these patients overcome their pain.

Fate made me cross paths with this angel who is making such a noble difference to the lives of those on a deathbed. We discussed a lot of things and in the course of that discussion, she happened to share a very touching incident of her life.

It so happened that once, an old couple walked into the hospital where Nirmala was working. The husband must have been around 80 and the wife around 75 years of age. The wife was suffering from advanced Leukaemia and required chemotherapy on a regular basis. Apart from that, there were also a few costly medicines that had been prescribed to control the disease. The couple couldn't have afforded hospital-stay and hence she was being treated as an out – patient, due to which they had to visit the hospital at regular intervals. During every visit, they both would come holding each other's hand firmly, taking slow steps to avoid breathlessness. The couple seemed tired but affectionately connected with each other.

On one such occasion, to soothe the old lady, Nirmala took time out and started chatting with her. She tenderly held the old lady's wrinkled, shrunken hands in her own and started consoling her with kind eyes and soft voice..

Nirmala said to the lady, "Mother, I can feel your pain in me! Have trust and faith in God. The best we can do is to surrender to His wishes and live a life of peace and calmness. He shall do only that what He feels is right for us. Pain and sufferings in our life are just a form of our prayer unto him."

In return, the old lady smiled at Nirmala, gently pulled her hands off and blessed her by placing her hands over Nirmala's head. Without uttering a word, the old lady spoke volumes through her eyes; the expressions on her wrinkled face were worth a thousand words. Tears rolled down the eyes of both ladies.

After a pause, Nirmala asked the old lady, "Mother, I have only seen your husband coming with you every time you visit the hospital. Where are your children and your relatives?"

The lady replied, "We don't have any close relatives. It is our misfortune that we were not blessed with a child. We both were Government employees and have been retired for more than a decade now. After retirement, it has only been the two of us for each other. We had been living this life happily supporting each other till I was diagnosed of cancer.

Nirmala asked her, "Mother, why don't you get admitted to the hospital and continue the treatment? It may do good for you. Travelling will only weaken you further."

At this, the lady responses, "My child, I think I can trust you with the real reason behind this decision of mine. But, you have to promise me that you will never tell this to my husband."

"I won't, Mother. You can trust me."

The lady disclosed, "We have been living our retired life only out of pension money that we are getting from the Government. It barely helps in making our ends meet. Hence, getting admitted in the hospital may not be affordable for us. I do not want to burden my husband, as, after me, he still has to continue out of his own pension amount. Second important reason is that, in his entire life, my husband has not made anything other than a cup of tea. He has always been very dependent on me for everything. It is utmost essential for me to go back home after every session. In this process, he has to take care of me and unknowingly, he is learning how to take care of himself and our home. He is learning to cook and my presence there also makes him comfortable while dong all these chores. Indirectly, I am preparing him to face life after I am gone. He has to live alone after me; he needs to be prepared, else he will just wither away."

Nirmala was left speechless listening to what the lady had said. It depicted the depth of love of the old lady towards her husband and the ability of hers to think beyond herself even at such a difficult phase of her life. Nirmala's eyes were filled with tears. Without realising, her tears started rolling down her eyes as she clasped the old lady's hand and kissed it with reverence.

Nirmala wanted to see how she could best help this old lady who was an epitome of love and thought of speaking to the lady's husband to see if she could be hospitalized for a better treatment. She approached the old man. He was sitting on a bench outside the ward, his body dwindling with the fear of the (un)expected but his eyes still flashing rays of hope. Nirmala made small talk with him to understand his psyche and make him feel comfortable. Then she came to the main topic saying, "I was just chatting with your beloved wife and as she is of my mother's age, I could see a reflection of my mother in her. I shall take care of her whenever she visits the hospital. I need to understand if it is possible for you to admit her to the hospital, so that we can take proper care of her. Her cancer is in an advanced stage and hence needs intensive care and continuous medication. If you agree, we can see what best can be done."

Overcome with emotion at Nirmala's kindness, the old man burst into tears. It was after a long time that someone was asking about them so kindly and offering to help them. Nirmala understood that his love for his wife was putting him in despair.

The old man covered up by saying that the medicines bill per month are so high that they couldn't afford them. Nirmala asked for the prescription sheet and went through it. It immediately struck her that the medicines prescribed were all branded ones which were very costly and if they could be replaced with generic versions of similar composition medicines, this would save a lot of money which in turn could be used for her hospitalization. Nirmala suggested this to the old man, showing him the possibility of self-funding for hospitalizing his wife.

However, he still refused to hospitalize her. Nirmala was perplexed and asked him the reason behind his decision. After much pursuing, the old man said to Nirmala, "I shall tell you my reasons, but only if you promise me that you will never let my wife know about this conversation."

Nirmala agreed.

The old man said, "I have multiple reasons behind not getting her hospitalized. Yes, even I know the generic version is cheaper as this was also mentioned to me by the doctor. However, I have noticed that the branded medicine is more soothing for my wife and hence I would not compromise on anything and deprive her of the best. As far as affording these medicines are concerned, our pension money is not sufficient to take care of this monthly bill. Even my wife is not aware that I have sold our house and have taken back the same house on rent from the investor who purchased it. I have kept the entire sale-money in my bank account so that atleast I am able to meet all the expenses that are required to take care of her treatment. The doctor had mentioned to me that she has only half a year to live and I do not want her to be confined within the four walls of the hospital ward during the last days of her life. I want her to walk around like a free bird till her last breath, I want her to spent time moving around the house that she has built with utmost care, I want her to get that inner happiness she is deriving out of preparing me to face life after her, I want her to be 'her' till her last breath! For that I shall make any sacrifice that is possible for me. After she leaves for her destined abode, I shall move to an old-age home and live the rest of my life with these fond memories of her."

Nirmala was shell-shocked after hearing the old man's reasons. This time she had no tears in her eyes, as she was in such an emotional jolt that even her body didn't know how to respond. She felt too numb to say anything. After a long time, she gathered courage to simply touch the old man's wrinkled palm that was completely wrinkled and shivering. She slowly got up and walked towards the ward. The old couple's face kept coming in front of her eyes again and again.

The true reciprocation of each other's love by both of them taught Nirmala that sacrifice is all about giving till it hurts and happily accepting it!!!

~~ ~~ ~~

Chapter 4

Equal Opportunities to All

After completing his studies and qualifying as MBBS & MD, Dr. Amit Chandran decides to join the corporate world of pharmaceuticals instead of following the usual track of etching a career in medicine. His aspiration is to be a part of research and development and thereby, help pharma companies make newer breakthroughs in medicine and therapy. Amit gets selected in a MNC pharma company. He undergoes structured and methodical training in the area of disease and its treatment.

Armed with his stellar education and training, Amit is equipped with the requisite skill and will to succeed in his chosen area. He prepares himself to enter the market to establish the need for the medicines that his company is selling. As the Head of Medical function, Amit decides to visit the field and work along with the field team and also conduct a CME

(Continuous Medical Examination) program for Doctors as a strategy towards educating and promoting the company medicines.

Amit selects a rural town in the state of Tamilnadu to start his field-work with a belief that it will help in achieving early success due to the lack of reach and awareness in that town. On his first day of field-work, Amit is totally charged and motivated. He meets his field representative and along with him, moves to meet the doctors. Amit completes four doctor visits and is convinced that his choice of the town was right; he can explain the need for the medicines and influence those doctors quite well.

In the evening, Amit is taken to a charitable hospital run by a trust where he is to conduct CME for the doctors. Amit ensures that all preparations are in place and finally rushes through his Powerpoint presentation that he is to share with the doctors. At the stipulated time, the CME is inaugurated by the chairman of the local doctors' association and Amit is invited to make the presentation. Amit gives an exemplary presentation. The doctors attending the session get answers to all their questions and all their concerns get fully addressed by Amit. As the session gets over, one of the attendees, Dr. Srinivas, approaches Amit and insists that he should meet the founder trustee of the hospital as this would help him in fostering relations in this town further. Amit willingly agrees.

After the dinner session with all the doctors, Amit and Srinivas excuse themselves and move towards the founder trustee's office. As Amit enters through the door, he observes that the office is a plush space decorated in tasteful style. It has white marble flooring and a beautifully done-up ceiling in sky blue colour. The walls are painted in mild lemon-yellow colour with pillars in orange. Beautiful paintings make the walls look more attractive. The curtains are of a lovely shade of brown and the air-conditioning has kept the room cool. Overall, the office has a lot of vibrancy and positive energy. In the centre of the office, is a single-seater sofa; two wooden chairs sit facing each other on either side of the sofa.

On the sofa, an old man aged around 70 is seated at ease. He is dressed in a simple white shirt and white mundu (traditional wear of Tamil Nadu). Nearly 20 persons standing, surrounding him to get his attention. Amit notices the old man addressing every person's concern with equal compassion and patience. Never once does his face crease in frowns. Never once does his voice get irritable. He ensures that every person is heard by him.

Amit stands close-by observing all this. Once all the people leave, Dr. Srinivas approaches the old man and gives him briefing of the day and also a brief introduction of Amit. The old man gets up from his seat and with hands folded in Namaste, greets Amit warmly, and makes him sit on a chair placed next to his. In all sophistication, Amit speaks to the old man in English. He introduces himself and then speaks about the vision of his company, the products they sell, the areas of therapy they cover and their aim for the next five years.

For some time, the old man gave Amit a polite hearing. After that he started getting restless. He asked Amit if he knew the local language, Tamil, and if so, could he speak in the same? Amit confessed that he could not speak Tamil, but he did understand it. Hearing this, the old man gave a sigh of relief and then he started talking: "My name is Gajapathy Iyer. I have only studied till 2nd standard. I do not understand English, hence it would be better if we spoke in Tamil."

Amit continued speaking in English, with Srinivas translating to the old man.

Amit exclaimed, "Sir, I am surprised to know this. You are the founder trustee of such a reputed charitable hospital and you are saying you are uneducated?"

Gajapathy replied, "Saar (addressing Amit with respect), I belonged to a poor family. My father use to make biscuits for living. He used to ride on a cycle with a trunk full of biscuits in the morning and travel from street to street to sell it. He couldn't have afforded my education, so I dropped out from school after studying 2 classes. I then started accompanying my father to all those places where he sold biscuits. I had seen him saving money on a daily basis. His habit of thrift enabled him so much that over the years, he employed four persons who would carry biscuits on cycles to various parts of the city to sell them. He then focused on manufacturing a variety of biscuits, taking special care to maintain quality. Not surprisingly, his sales sky-rocketed. By the time I was 15 years old, we had a small factory of 15 to 20 workers to manufacture biscuits. My mother used to take care of the factory employees by providing them tea, snacks and lunch. She would also organize lunch tiffins for the sales persons. My father focused on quality of the products but he also took care of the 20 sales persons who continued travelling to various parts of the city to sell the biscuits. By then, we also had cakes and sweets to sell. But the focus was still on door-to-door delivery sales. I was one of the sales person travelling on cycle to sell our products. I was covering that part of the city which was predominantly covered by slums. I travelled daily on cycle to that slum area and sold our products there. I closely saw and experienced the lives of the people there - the compromise on hygiene, lack of water, electricity, sanitation, etc. The children there were deprived of education because their parents could not afford to educate them. They led a very hand-to-mouth existence in a city where people had so much money to spend for luxuries but not for uplifting their own brothers and sisters in the slum. This touched me deeply. I wanted to do something for the deprived. I decided that it's my moral responsibility to become rich through the right efforts and sources, so that I could give back to the society. I sincerely focused on the business and helped my father grow it even more. We ventured into opening outlets and selling our products through them. The profits were ploughed back to increase production capacity. However, in spite of earning so much, we continued our simple living and ensured we only carried back home what we required for our daily living. Our business kept growing; we had a chain of outlets and franchises. We automated our manufacturing and opened manufacturing sites at three different places. At my age of 42, I had a successful business model. We took the business forward by further integrating it into surface transportation and in a span of 10 years, we had a fleet of trucks running across the country which not only catered to our business needs, but also generated its own business and helped earn better profits.

By the age of 52, after having ensured sustained success and growth of our business, I felt the urge of devoting my life to making difference in the lives of others. Hence, I handed over the business responsibilities to my son and daughter; today they handle the business with same level of passion that my father and I had. As per what I had decided long back, I formed a trust consisting of my trusted friends who were with me in my journey since my age of 15. They also shared my dream. We bought land and built a school as my focus was on uplifting the children towards a bright future by providing them with free education. My next aim was to provide affordable medication to those who couldn't manage paying huge bills of private hospitals and hence we build this hospital. We have been running this as a charitable hospital at a very nominal cost, to help poor patients recover from their ailments faster and better. For the past 20 years, I have been only working towards helping poor people get a better quality of living. They lovingly call me "Thatha" (Grand-father) and that's my biggest wealth that I have earned in my life!!"

Amit was stunned to hear all this. He found it unbelievable that such a successful and influential personality beheld so much humility within himself.

Gajapathy continued: "Saar, if I, an uneducated person could do all this in my life, you are so highly educated. Imagine how much more you can do with your life for yourself and for the society? You have much more power in yourself to bring about even more change!!"

Amit was left spellbound on hearing this. He folded his hands together in respect to Thatha, took his blessings and slowly walked out of the room. As he was distancing himself from Gajapathy, his mind threw waves of questions for which he had to seek an answer. His intrusive mind was predominantly inquiring why he couldn't do all that what Gajapathy could do and what curtails his ability in doing it? Amit was completely restless with these thoughts as he walked towards the street completely unaware of the surroundings, his turbulent mind still trying to find answers.

Finally, Amit realised that his inability probably had a lot to do with our education system. We are all taught how to compete with each other and score higher marks than the rest. We are not taught the skills of entrepreneurship, we are not taught risk-taking and we are not taught about social responsibility towards the society. Education first gets us into a competitive mode of scoring higher marks; it gets us better jobs after competing with other candidates; it makes us slaves towards earning better salary and a comfortable life. It certainly gets us a living but in return, has taken away the charm of life to see beyond, to take risks in life, to care for others!! It also answers why an entrepreneur can see through the business opportunities and have a better vision and create multiple employability options for all educated; whereas, we educated people are only chasing better jobs and better pay and protecting our own family. Once in this race, our focus gets narrowed only towards I, me and my family, we gradually lose our intrinsic capabilities of doing things differently and caring for others. As the stakes increase every year through increments, beyond a point we are unwilling to let go of the so called invincible imaginary boundary of security that we carry around us even when we are in the community.

We end up becoming a bird in the cage that was born to fly, but the comforts of the cage has made us forget our capabilities.

Probably if we are taught at an early age the ability of risk taking, caring for others and doing something worth for the community, the stakes at that age would be lesser and hence we shall surely end up creating more leaders than managers, and such leaders who can contribute to the society than the managers who consume the society!!!

~~ ~~ ~~

Chapter 5

Thanksgiving

Anamika was an authoritative and ambitious Senior Executive in a MNC Company. She led a beautiful, happy life with a successful career and blissful motherhood to two daughters, seven-year old Varsha and five year-old Prerna.

Anamika took utmost care of her daughters. As a single parent, she provided all that the little girls wanted, while also taking care to groom them to be self-sufficient and self-reliant. She taught her daughters how to lend a hand in household tasks, how to take care of themselves etc. She was particular about minute things like having breakfast and dinner together, so that they could mingle well as a family and also share their daily life with each other.

However, as it sometimes happens, this happiness did not last for long. Misfortune struck Anamika when, during a routine medical check-up, she is diagnosed with leukaemia of an advanced stage. This brings a sudden pause in the happy lives of all three.

Anamika is advised immediate hospitalization for further medication and progress observation. Being the strong lady that she is, Anamika is determined to fight through this situation. In the hospital, even when she is under treatment, she spends time with other patients and tries to console them and cheer them up convincing that life is a matter of living and not dying before death!!

Anamika makes friends with everyone in the ward, as well as, with the hospital staff. Nurses spend their free time with her to hear from her about the transformed perception about life and how they need to be full of energy all the time. Soon, the trust between them grows so much that they even approach Anamika seeking advice for their family problems.

Anamika's cousin sister, Prajakta was one person who would visit Anamika regularly every evening, bringing along Varsha and Prerna as well. Anamika would spend her evening time chatting with her daughters, asking them about their daily chore, progress in the school, about their friends and so on. During this conversation, she ensured to maintain a sense of touch all the time with her daughters, either through making their hair, or making the younger one sit on her lap and allowing the elder one to feed her mother. The family was complete when all three were together and Prajakta played a vital role of getting the trio together every day without fail. Prajakta also took great care of the children and her face always had an expression of deep concern for Anamika.

The other patients and nurses used to gossip about the family. One question foremost on everyone's mind was: 'where is Anamika's husband? Why isn't he visiting her?' But they never asked her about this as they did not want to hurt Anamika's sentiments. Anamika's hospital bills were paid by Prajakta all the time. Couple of times Prajakta's husband, Sandeep, also visited Anamika along with her daughters.

Days went by and it was exam time for both the daughters. The mother in Anamika was so concerned that she used to take their studies from her hospital bed and wish her daughters all the best for their exams. Next day she used to reconfirm the answers written by Varsha and Prerna, and later take revision for the next day's test. The entire process depicted care, concern, love and respect within the three. All this used to happen in the presence of Prajakta, who kept herself busy cutting fruits or preparing the spread of food that she brought for Anamika.

The mutual love and affection of this family and the selfless service of Prajakta towards this family was an astonishing sight for everyone in the ward including the nurses and the doctors.

Anamika's condition was deteriorating day by day, but the cheerfulness on her face was always alive. With each passing day, her spiritual connect to God was also magnifying. She spent more time in praying - not for herself, but for her daughters and other patients in the hospital. She encouraged everyone in her ward for a group prayer together in the evening as a way of expressing thanks to God for having kept them alive for one additional day!!! She firmly believed that when everyone joined hands and prayed together, blessings descended.

Few weeks passed by. Now Anamika's restlessness could be seen in her weak body, but there was a complete calmness on her face. She had instructed Prajakta not to get her daughters along as she didn't want them to see her plight. However, she continuously kept inquiring about her daughters with Prajakta. Understanding that her end was nearby, she requested Prajakta and Sandeep to arrange for a lawyer, as she expressed her desire to get her Will prepared. Sandeep got a lawyer within two days' time; this gentleman sat beside Anamika to get her Will made. Anamika got her entire property transferred equally to both her daughters and made Prajakta and Sandeep the trustees of the property till her daughters grew old enough to handle these assets. Prajakta assured Anamika that she would love both the kids like her own daughters and take care of them the same way as Anamika did. Anamika heaved a sigh of relief after this and then devoted her entire time in serving others and in prayers, but silently suffered the pain within without expressing it.

Finally, a day came when Anamika got completely confined to her bed and she was even unable to get up. She stopped responding to all medicines and treatment. Prajakta realized that her end is coming near and so requested Anamika if she wanted to see her daughters, but Anamika refused by saying "those are your daughters now and do take care of them. I do not want to be seen in such a miserable status by those little angels. Let me be a sweet memory in their lives!!"

The soul within Anamika's body was struggling to let loose and on one evening the last signs were clearly visible. Prajakta and Sandeep were immediately called by the hospital authorities and they reached as early as they could. Anamika could hold her breath till her beloved sister reached her. Prajakta lifted Anamika's dropping head, carefully moved it to her lap and started rubbing her hand over Anamika's shoulder. Prajakta had tears rolling down and few drops were falling over Anamika's face. Anamika's face held a mixed expression of pain and relief. In her sinking voice she inquired about her daughters and pressed Prajakta's palm gently to express her thanks and trust. With few long breaths and God's name on her lips, Anamika bid goodbye to all the people surrounding her bed by then. Everyone was in tears - the patients in the ward, the hospital staff, Prajakta and Sandeep. A good soul had departed from among every one whom she loved immensely.

Sandeep moved out of the ward as he couldn't stand the sorrow. As he stood near a pillar consoling himself, Dr. Amruta who had been attending to Anamika, approached him. She gently tapped on Sandeep's shoulder and requested him "You may please call Anamika's relatives and I also request you to start the documentation and other necessary process to carry her body home".

In a painful tone, Sandeep replied, "Yes Doctor, Prajakta and I need to complete the formalities and we request the hospital staff's co-operation in helping us get the process completed."

Dr. Amruta's curiosity got the better of her as she asked Sandeep, "Didn't Anamika have any other relatives? Where is her husband and other family members?"

Having kept everything bottled in himself for so long, Sandeep now lets his heart out in response to Amruta's question. He tells her, "Doctor, Anamika's life story is a strange one. Let me tell you in short. Anamika was an adopted child of Prajakta's maternal uncle. That noble man brought up Anamika like his own daughter and gave her the best of education, ingrained excellent values in her and also loved her very much. When he passed away, he transferred his entire property to Anamika. Anamika loved her foster father so immensely that she couldn't cope with the vacuum that was caused in her life after he left for his heavenly abode. As a thanks giving, she wanted to pay back this good deed of such a noble person. She decided not to marry and dedicated her life towards bringing up an orphaned child. Sometime later, Anamika read about a tragic incident that happened with a famer's family in a remote village, where the farmer committed suicide due to outstanding loans which he couldn't repay. That farmer was survived by two daughters, aged four years and two years. Anamika immediately travelled to that village and decided to adopt these girls. She got all the legal formalities completed. She brought the little girls with her and took care of them like her own daughters. She got them admitted to the best school and gave them all that a parent could think of for their children. Now, when Anamika has departed, she has left everything to these two children and entrusted such a huge responsibility on me and Prajakta. We are honoured that Anamika trusted us and we are blessed to be the chosen ones. We shall now ensure that Anamika's dreams for her daughters are fulfilled through us!!

Dr. Amruta was in a thrall listening to such a sensitive love-filled story of Anamika's life and her manner of thanksgiving.

Every good deed makes a life pure and all such pure lives dedicate themselves to good deed. This is one way of offering our prayers to our loving God!!!

~~ ~~ ~~

Chapter 6

Understanding the Divine

Anila was a fresh graduate out of college. Unlike other girls from the college who were bubbling with enthusiasm to embrace life, Anila was timid, withdrawn, and especially worried about her career. She was a very reserved student who was staying so far at a girl's hostel. After her graduation, without wasting time, Anila starts hunting for a job.

Soon, she gets an offer from a private company for the post of Executive (Administration) and willingly takes up the job as she has to manage her finances on her own. She firmly believes in her own capabilities and doesn't want to be a burden on her parents by demanding money for her expenses. Her first job salary is just sufficient enough to make the ends meet and with this thought, she carries on in her life.

Her employees place a lot of expectations on Anila. However she repeatedly falters in her assigned tasks and makes silly mistakes time and again. Her superior gets annoyed with her careless approach and warns her of disciplinary action if she is unable to cope up with the work. Yet, matters remain the same over the next six months and Anila's manager gets frustrated correcting her mistakes and becoming answerable for Anila's errors. Anila is confronted by her manager and is warned that this matter will be escalated to the higher level. Anila's report reaches Prashant, the Head of the Department. Prashant studies the report of Anila's progress. Instead of reacting to the observations listed in the report, Prashant decides to give a hearing to Anila. On an appointed time one Friday evening, Anila reaches Prashant's office with lot of apprehension and a readily made resignation letter in her bag, thinking that in case the discussion concludes towards a termination, she would rather resign and leave the organisation.

Once inside the office, Prashant makes Anila feel comfortable and starts the discussion.

He says, "Anila, you must be aware why you have been called here. Let me clarify to you, I am not at all interested in discussing those observations in the report nor want to seek any justification from you. You have been in the system for the past eight months and I hardly could get time to know you. Do share whatever you want to let me know about you, but apart from work related matters. We shall deal with work matters later."

Anila was perplexed as this discussion was not in her scheme of expectations!! She didn't know what to speak and from where to start. She stared at Prashant's face and could see calm and composed Prashant with a smile on his lips and compassion in his eyes.

Looking at his kind face, Anila felt emboldened to speak. She replied, "Sir, I come from a lower middle class family. My father has struggled all his life to provide us with bare necessities and also take care of my education. My younger sister is studying and is with my parents at my native place. I wanted to make a successful career and hence decided to pursue my studies in a metro. Hereby, after completing my studies I have taken up a job in this city itself. I don't want to return to my home town as it is not providing me sufficient opportunities to grow. I stay here alone in a rented flat and am capable of managing all my work alone. I hardly have any friends and also do not enjoy mingling with people much. I want to just focus on my work and my life."

There was a short pause and a silence after Anila spoke in haste, encapsulating whatever she wanted to speak. Prashant could sense some pain in her tone and realised that Anila was withholding something.

He said, "I appreciate the efforts put in by your father to ensure both his daughters are educated. It depicts his love and care for his daughters. I also appreciate your self-confidence and will-power in managing your life on your own terms at such a young age. However, I would like to understand one thing from you. What is it that disturbs you the most and distracts your attention?"

Anila was confused with this question and in spontaneity exclaimed, "The only thing that disturbs me the most is my mother's relation with me!"

Prashant asked her, "I can't understand how your mother disturbs you the most. Can you elaborate?"

Anila replied, "My mother never loved me. She always treated me with disrespect. I can quote many instances that I have registered in my mind."

Prashant : "You should not be holding hatred against your mother. Anyhow, just let me know any two instances where you felt your mother doesn't love you, so that I can understand the situation better."

Anila : "During my school days, I have seen that when my friends had some issue at the school, their mothers always defended their daughters, but in my case, my mother would always let me down. I was always blamed for everything and my mother would ask me to apologise to others. This had a severe bearing on my self-confidence and I started withdrawing myself from others!!! My friends' mothers would always help them with their homework, but for me, no such help was available. Whenever I approached my mother, she would insist I should do my homework on my own and even if it meant getting a remark from the school, she would still insist I should do my work on my own. She never supported me in my growing years and hence I had decided that once I am able to be on my own, I shall never stay with my mother and live my life on my own terms!!"

Anila's intelligence couldn't comprehend the depth of the emotions she was experiencing and it gave way to tears rolling down her eyes. Prashant sat in complete silence, allowing Anila to speak up freely and vent her emotions out.

After a long pause, Prashant said, "Anila, my child, understand God's way of preparing us. As Sadhu Vaswani says, 'God upsets our plans so that he can execute his plan for us through us and his plans for us are always right!!' Your mother is just an instrument in the hands of God. She is doing what is destined for you. You were to live your life alone in the coming years and it would have been very difficult if you were entangled in the care of relations. It would have been further worse if you wouldn't have known how to take care of yourself. Your mother was preparing you for the days ahead in your life. Instead of having gratitude towards her for what she was preparing you for, you are carrying hatred for her? Today you wouldn't have managed your life all alone in a busy metro unless that will-power was developed within you and that could have been possible only because of your mother!!! If you believe today you can develop wings for yourself to fly, do remember that these wings are courtesy your mother and for this, you must forgive her. You have been holding hatred against her since your school days. This will only harm you as you can never move up in life with roots of hatred. They will never allow you to settle in whatever you are doing. Focus is the crucial aspect of life and in your case, your core focus is to prove your mother wrong!! Forgive your mother, as you require to liberate yourself from this self-destructive thought. Be thankful to God for having given you such a mother who made you strong enough to face any situation in life."

Anila was in meditative silence and had a glare on her face after listening to this positive side of her life and the novel thought accompanying it. After some time, she touched Prashant's palm with a sense of gratitude. Her eyes were still filled, but now it was with tears of happiness. There had been a paradigm shift in the way she looked at her life. She thanked Prashant and walked out of his office.

As a follow-up towards this discussion, Prashant inquired about Anila on Monday morning and he was informed that Anila has taken leave and shall report on Tuesday.

On Tuesday morning, as Prashant enters his office, he is surprised to see Anila waiting for him in his cabin. Anila wishes him and hands over a small token of gift to Prashant, stating that this is from her mother to him.

Anila: "After hearing from you, I thought over it the entire Friday night. I couldn't resist anymore and hence on Saturday morning, I took the first bus to my native place and went straight home. On seeing my mother, I simply hugged her and cried. In return, she hugged me tight. I could feel that warmth in her hug and she also reciprocated in the same manner. We felt complete as mother and daughter for the first time in our life. I am blessed, thanks to you. My mother is the happiest person as her daughter has grown up to understand life in a larger perspective. I owe all this only to you and this small gift is from my mother to you for having filled her life with happiness by getting her daughter back. Sir, I promise you I shall not be the same person anymore. I shall always hold you in high respect and prove you right."

Anila kept her word. She changed herself so much that everyone could notice the pleasant shift in her. She mingled with everyone in office, her attention span towards work improved. She became more helpful to others and always gave importance to others' views.

One year from then on, Anila was adjudged the Best Employee of the company. In her thanksgiving speech, she said, "Everyone strives through difficulties in life, but analysing them and seeing every challenge as an opportunity and moving ahead in life is possible only through a well-wisher who can show you that GOD is always with you especially during your bad times to take you through. This organisation is blessed with such a person called Prashant Sir!!! Thank you, Sir; for making me walk on the right path in life!!!"

Life is a matter of living in Gratitude towards the Divine.

~~~ ~~~ ~~~

Chapter 7

Coincidence

This is a story of six young boys who were best of friends staying in the same locality. These adolescents enjoyed being together and playing pranks on the neighbours and other people. They would go to any extent to play their tricks and this included even their parents. They would suddenly decide to go for a swim in the nearby river without informing anyone and return late in the evening, making their parents anxious about their children's whereabouts.

Few such instances are worth a mention to understand to what extent they could go to have such mere fun for themselves at the cost of pain of others.

The youngsters used to meet every day after dinner and spend a couple of hours together wandering on the streets. They would observe people on the streets and plan something naughty depending on who they chanced upon. During one winter, they observed that one middle-aged person who had a farm field nearby would put together some dry sticks and leaves and burn them up in the night to get warmth from the fire. He would do this every night. One day, these six friends got together with their prank act and a plan. They met early, collected some pebbles and climbed up a tree close to where this man used to light the fire. They waited there till the man started his routine and as the fire was set up and the man was relaxing near it, they started throwing pebbles on the fire-lit sticks. It created a commotion with fire particles spreading in the air all around. The poor man didn't understand what was happening and out of fear he ran into the fields, lost his balance and fell there. The boys silently climbed down the tree and went home, having had their share of laughter and fun of having disturbed one more person's peace.

During Diwali, they would usually unite together for giving trouble to others. During they day, they would tactfully slip in a metal coin between the socket and the bulb placed inside the kandil (lamp) of their neighbour's house and in the night, enjoy the fun of the fuse getting blown out when the neighbours put on the kandil. They would tilt the rockets (crackers) and burn them in a way such that the burnt rocket would hit somebody's house and the boys would run away after that.

Once, they observed that there was a Tantrik baba (a person who does black magic) nearby their area and he did lot of havans (offerings) and sacrificial acts to please the demon gods. Now, these six wanted to test their ability with this Tantrik as well. Again their corrupt minds knitted a plan together. They went to a slaughter house, bought skulls of 2 buffaloes and cleaned them up. They arranged for some lemons, red and yellow colour powder and made two hardboard cut-outs of tiger footprints. One night when it was pitch dark, they went to the Tantrik's house at around 2.00 am and started executing their dirty plan. They wrapped the skulls in blood-like colour and placed them at the front door of the house. Then, they laid the tiger foot-marks all around outside the house and even on the walls. They spread and sprinkled red and yellow colour powder across the outer walls of the house to depict that some evil act had been performed to transpire some omen. After all this, they slipped out of the place and returned home to sleep.

Next morning, they sent someone to visit the Tantrik's house and get an update. The news was most encouraging for them, as they had been triumphant in establishing fear in the Tantrik's mind. The Tantrik was not sure what kind of black magic was this, as he has never learnt such a magic where skulls of buffalos were used and foot marks of tigers were found all across and colours of blood were scattered all over. He could only infer it as, that some evil was going to happen to him through wild animals and they would tear him apart. With this fear, he decided to move out and change his place. The boys rejoiced and were happy in their own world being victorious and adding one more mischievous achievement to their list.

On one such occasion of their daily chores and planning their next prank, they observed that one person who was a mill employee staying in their same locality returned home every night at 11.00 pm after completing his second shift. This person had a routine that after entering his house he would put on the kitchen light, finished his dinner and would then come out of the house. He would go to one corner near his house where it was covered with bushes, stand there smoking a cigarette and then go back home to sleep. The boys decided to make this hapless person their next target.

They came up with another innovative destructive plan. They decided to scare him with a ghost make-over. That night they started the preparations. They applied sticky white colour adhesive on the face of one of them and once it was dried, pulled it out partially to make the face look scratchy and scary. They coloured this face mask white. The boy was then equipped with a dark coloured bed sheet and a torch.

The plan was that this boy would hide near the bushes covering himself with the bed sheet. Once the man entered his house and later, comes out as per routine, the boy would stand up with only his face exposed and torch light held from below his chin reflecting on his face. He would then call out the man's name in a scary tone.

They practiced it to see the impact and it was indeed frightening. The plan was fool-proof. The boy on act took his position, with the other five boys keeping an eye over the entire act from a distance. As usual at 11.15 pm, the man came out and the rest of the incidence unfolded as planned!!

It was dark all around and the boy waiting near the bushes got up with the torch light on, reflecting his masked face and in a scary low tone voice asking

"Ganpat, kaisa hey re tu?" (Ganpat, how are you?). The man got bewildered and yelled so loudly crying for help that the boy got scared! In that muddle, he caught hold of the man's hand firmly. Alas, the man fainted then and there!!!

The boy didn't know what to do next and ran away from the scene. Seeing all this, the other five also decided to do a vanishing act. However, at the last minute, one of them decided otherwise and with an intent to help that man, ran towards him. Seeing this, the other four followed him, as they wanted to be together. They reached out to the man, picked him up and took him inside his house. One boy ran to get some water, while another ran to call a doctor, as the man was still unconscious. The man's family members were scared and concerned; at the same time they were thankful for the good gesture of these boys. They had no clue that it was these boys itself who were responsible for this entire episode.

The doctor arrived in next ten minutes. By then, the man had come to his conscious state, but was unable to speak to anyone due to the shock of such a horrifying experience. The doctor checked his blood pressure and pulse. He told the man to relax and not to worry about anything, prescribed some medicines, collected his fees and left.

The boys were feeling very guilty about the entire episode, knowing very well that they were close to killing someone for mere fun of theirs!! The guilt prick was urging them to apologise and clarify the truth to the man. One of the boys took the initiative and in order to start a conversation, asked the man as to what exactly happened that he got so scared?

The man said, "Today while coming back from work, I got down at the railway station at around 10.45 pm. The platform was empty and only three-four persons got down from the train. As I was walking towards my house, I saw a lady standing outside the railway platform with her son, may be 3-year old, holding her hand. Out of curiosity, I asked her what she was doing in such a lonely place at such a time and could I be of any help to her? She told me that she wanted to go to her parents' place but had no idea how to reach there, as she was visiting them after five years. This confused me, because how could anybody forget their parent's place, even after five years back? I asked her where the place is. She mentioned the name of the place which was on my way itself. I told her that I was going the same way and if she could follow me, I could show her the place. She agreed and along with her son, started following me. On the way, I picked up conversation with her asking why she had come alone with her son and where was her husband? She said that her husband beat her a lot and tired of it she and her son had left the house. I asked her, in that case you should have come in the day to your parents' place; why did you come in the night? She replied that 'my marriage was a love marriage and my parents never recognized it. Hence, I had to go through all my sufferings alone without any support. Now my relation with my husband has worsened and in this situation, I have no place to go. I have been waiting for my parents' acceptance for the past one year'. Now I was getting more confused. So, I further inquired, 'if so, what were you doing in the last five years and why have you come searching for your parents today and that too, at such an odd time in the night?' She replied that 'I have been seeking their acceptance for the past four years since marriage, but they never recognized it. My husband also didn't treat me and my son well and my life was turning miserable. One year back, the fight with my husband took an ugly shape and finally it all came to an end. Since then, for the last one year every night I try to tell my story to someone who can understand my pain and reach out to my parents and convey to them my throbbing, as I am now unable to communicate directly with them'. I was completely overwhelmed at what she said. With curiosity, I asked, 'why have you selected me to communicate this to your parents?' She said, I can see on your face that you are going through some deep pain in life and I only approach such persons, as they can understand my pain and empathize with me. Maybe one such person can reach out to my parents and tell them that their daughter was not wrong and that she always loved her parents. In return she wants their love so that she can be liberated'.

These words of hers shook me to the roots. Continuing my walk, I looked down and could see only my shadow. There was no shadow of the lady and the child. Petrified, I looked around and suddenly there was no one. Out of that fear, I reached home and had my dinner thinking about the incident and also about, why had she chosen me? Later, as I came out still thinking about that incident, she appeared again - this time in form of a ghost and asking me how am I? I just fainted and don't know anything after that."

The boys were completely perplexed. They had no words!!! They left the place in silence, internalizing what they had just heard.

The realization they got that day was that ' just for our own fun, we have been distressing others' peace, not realizing how much pain is there in everyone's life; and what circumstances they might be going through. We were being utterly selfish just to play pranks on such persons'. Next day morning they gathered together but no one was talking. There was complete silence as there was a volcano inside each one of them waiting to erupt!! It was the moment of awakening. When they spoke, the words were of wisdom. They united to take an oath on how they could be of use to others and decided to commit themselves to the cause of helping others.

The boys were ready for an awakening, making a significant difference in the life of others through them. Almighty has his own ways of emerging and handholding everyone to the purpose of his/her life!!!

Chapter 8

Understanding Religion

Padmanabhan is a faithful devotee of Lord Ayyappa (incarnation of Lord Vishnu & Lord Shiva) and he instils similar faith in his sons Sandeep and Arjun. Due to need of a job and earning for living, few years back, Padmanabhan moves to Dubai and settles there with his family. In spite of this, he makes an annual pilgrimage to Sabrimala, the abode of Lord Ayyappa, without fail.

To provide a brief insight about Sabarimala: it is a place of pilgrimage in Pathanamtitta District of Kerala. The temple is open only five days every month during February to October. From November to January, it is the festive season and the temple is open continuously. Devotees visiting the temple have to go through a 41-days penance and after following certain prescribed rituals, have to visit Sabarimala and climb a distance of 7 ½ kms of the Sabarimala mountain barefoot. While climbing, they have to carry on their head an erumudikettu (auspicious sack containing offerings for the Lord) and while climbing, continue chanting the Lord's name in devotion and ultimate surrender to Him. It is a sacred journey for the devotees and the nirvana that they experience on getting one glimpse of the Lord is unparalleled. Devotees wait for the next season to go through the same process for that one moment of connect with the Lord and pray for such spiritual connect with the Lord every year.

Padmanabhan had made it a ritual to visit Sabarimala every year and also to get along with him his sons. By now, Sandeep was 20 and Arjun was 18 years old. All three travelled from Dubai to Cochin by flight. From there, they went by train to the nearest railway station, Chengannoor and continued their journey towards experiencing the movement of ecstasy in surrender to their Lord. After their prayer and offerings to the Lord, the satisfied spiritual souls returned their way back and reached the nearest railway station for their onward journey towards Cochin airport. As the trains were running late, Sandeep and Arjun ventured outside the railway station to the nearby market while Padmanabhan waited at the station. They had two hours of waiting; so, the boys went window shopping and roaming around the market. Sandeep was interested in some decorative items in one of the shop and he stopped by to pick up a few, whereas Arjun went ahead in that crowded market not realizing that Sandeep was not with him. Nearly two hours had passed and Sandeep realized that it was time to return. He looked around for Arjun, but Arjun was not there. Presuming Arjun must have gone back, Sandeep rushed to the station. Here at the station, the train had already arrived and Padmanabhan was anxious as the boys had not returned. The train started leaving the platform and since the boys hadn't returned, Padmanabhan didn't enter the train. Suddenly he saw Sandeep rushing towards the platform yelling, "Dad get in, I will catch the train". Padmanabhan presumed Arjun must be following. He picked up the luggage and jumped into the compartment of the moving train; Sandeep also managed to catch the last compartment. At the next station, Sandeep managed to change the compartment and reach out to his father. When Padmanabhan enquired about Arjun with Sandeep, he was shocked, as he had presumed Arjun must be with dad. That is when they both realized that Arjun was left out and they did not have any trace of him. Arjun's luggage was with Padmanabhan and hence Arjun had no money or any identity document with him. This scared them further and they immediately got down the train and proceeded back to Chengannoor railway station, where this entire incident had occurred. They went around the market to trace Arjun, but returned with no luck. They went to the railway station and filed a missing-person complaint with the Railway

Police as well as with the State Police. They took a lodging room for two days with a hope of getting back Arjun, but all efforts failed. Finally, Padmanabhan and Sandeep had to leave back for Dubai due to the exigencies of work and studies. Padmanabhan called his brother, who resided in Trichur, to follow up with the police to trace Arjun. Bestowing this responsibility upon his brother, Padmanabhan and his son Sandeep left for Dubai with a hope that the police department would continue their search for Arjun and would soon get him back.

However, what had in fact happened that unfortunate day with Arjun was that, as he was wandering around, he lost his way and later when he realized that he would be getting late for the train, started hastily rushing back without knowing the direction. In this hurry and confusion, he landed in front of a speeding car that dashed him and Arjun was thrown off the road and he landed hitting his head. The impact of the accident was so much that Arjun fell unconscious. The driver of the car got terribly scared and in a haste he lifted Arjun, pulled him inside the car and drove him down straight to Wayanad where he was heading to. There at Wayanad, this driver left the bleeding Arjun in front of a church and vanished. The pastor of that church was alarmed to see a bleeding young person lying in front of the church and he immediately got him rushed to the hospital. There,

Arjun was treated and taken care of. He regained his consciousness after two days of struggling for his life. However, the impact of the accident on his head made him lose his memory and the doctors termed this state as "temporary memory loss syndrome" or temporary amnesia. The pastor took pity on this boy and gave him shelter at his home under his supervision and medical treatment. To connect him with a name, the pastor named him Anthony.

Anthony spent his day learning under the gifted guidance of the pastor. Anthony was an obedient boy and he participated in various activities of the church. He first took interest in gardening and helped the gardener; then he took interest in the orphanage administered by the church and took care of the love-starved children in the orphanage. Anthony was a loving person and he cared for all the children and they also reciprocated in the same manner towards him. Considering the compassion Anthony showed towards the children, the pastor put him in-charge of the administration of the orphanage. Anthony worked towards the betterment of the children and became their benefactor. Over a period of time, Anthony also learned the teachings from the holy book "Bible" and with the understanding of those teachings, helped the children unfold the understandings of the parables better, align themselves to live for larger interest, have self-belief and also understand that God is always with them. He devoted ten years of his life in this noble work.

Anthony was now nearing 30 years of age. He was a much-loved person by all in the community and grew up as pride of the church and especially of the pastor who had given him a new lease of life. Life was going in peace and harmony for Anthony; but he could never understand one thing. Whenever he saw a group of devotees in black dress on their way to Sabarimala, an inner voice always urged him to join hands and pray along with them. He could never understand what this connection was. He expressed this to the pastor, who in turn recommended him not to have disturbance in life as it yields nothing other than pain, and to instead focus on what his heart and mind says is right. Anthony could neither comprehend nor ever act on this.

Once he expressed to the pastor that he would like to visit this holy place of Sabarimala and experience the satisfaction towards his inner cry that he could never understand. He wanted to know what was connecting him to Lord Ayyappa of Sabarimala. The pastor being a noble man and broad minded, willingly allowed Anthony to prepare for this holy expedition. Anthony searched for a Guruswami (the group leader) under whom he could learn the processes and reach Sabarimala. Anthony was blessed in his search, for, a noble person accepted him in his group and also hand-held him to understand the processes. Then the day arrived when Anthony had to start his journey to Sabarimala. They hired a car from Wayanad to Sabarimala and started their journey. Anthony meticulously followed all the rituals and along with his Guruswami reached Sabarimala, the heavenly abode of Lord Ayyappa. He climbed the mountain barefoot, reached the pinnacle, climbed the auspicious 18 steps, crossed the entrance of the temple and reached in front of the altar. His joy had no bounds standing there and worshipping the lord with both hands joined over the head and chanting the name of the lord, "Swamiyee Sharanam Ayyappa".

Later, reflecting on this experience, he could feel immense serenity and peace within himself for having worshiped and seen the Lord. His eyes were filled with tears and heart filled with faith. It was now time to climb down the mountain and he and his Guruswami started their journey back. They reached near the base of the Sabarimala mountain and commenced their journey back to Wayanad by car. On the way, they halted for lunch at Ernakulum. As the car was getting parked, Anthony got down from the wrong side not realizing there was a car speeding just behind. Anthony was hit by the car and he fell on the road. His Guruswami rushed to save him and pulled him off the road. By then, Anthony was unconscious. The Guruswami hurried him to a nearby hospital. There

Anthony was treated and he regained consciousness after a couple of hours.

After he gained consciousness, the doctors were startled, as Anthony now was no more Anthony, but Arjun! This Arjun remembered everything that had happened to him till the age of 20, but couldn't remember anything of the past 10 years. He even couldn't recognize the Guruswami! Due to the shock of the accident, Arjun had regained his memory of the past, as if suddenly someone has connected the long closed memory lane, but by shutting the present continuous memory. Arjun could precisely remember the address of Dubai where he resided, he remembered his mother, father and brother Sandeep, the telephone number and so on. However, the telephone number he provided wasn't the latest number as technology had evolved over past 10 years and everything had changed. Through Facebook, the doctors could locate Sandeep and found his telephone number. They tried contacting Sandeep at his Dubai number. The person who attended the phone communicated to the doctors that Sandeep and his parents were travelling to India and currently they were in Kerala. The person also gave Sandeep's local mobile number to the doctor. This was a mere coincidence, as the entire family was in Kerala, at Trichur - merely a two-hour drive away from where this hospital was. The Doctor called up Sandeep to communicate and confirm if whatever Arjun had said was right. The intention was to help Arjun find his relatives. On hearing this, Sandeep was thrilled! He just couldn't control his emotions and burst out in tears. Sandeep immediately communicated this information to his parents. For them, it was like finding a long-lost treasure found and in this eagerness, they immediately started for the hospital. In a short time, they reached the hospital.

Time had made lot of changes in Sandeep and Arjun, but Arjun could immediately identify his parents and stretched his arms towards them like a small child!! Arjun's mother held his hand and kissed his forehead. There were tears rolling down everyone's eyes and dripping down over the cheeks. The parents had found their lost son and the son had got back the entire family. The Guruswami blessed Arjun, congratulated the parents and with a smiling face walked out with an expression that he had completed the task assigned to him by the Lord.

The Doctors recommended few days of rest for Arjun, after which he could be discharged from the hospital. As Arjun was resting, he was updated by his parents and Sandeep about all that had happened in the family in the last 10 years and kept on inquiring with him whether he remembered anything of this time, but for Arjun, it was like the world had stopped 10 years back. It was a complete dark patch of a decade which he couldn't recollect. Padmanabhan, Arjun's dad also told him that their purpose of visit to India this time was to finalise a match for Sandeep's wedding and they had to travel to Bangalore, where the girl resides. They had come to Trichur to their family house and from there, they would be travelling by road to Bangalore. He also requested Arjun to join them. After conducting a complete check-up, the doctors agreed to discharge Arjun from the hospital, so that he could travel with his family to Bangalore.

After two days, they commenced the journey from Trichur to Bangalore by road in two SUV vehicles consisting of a group of 10 people - Sandeep's family and six other relatives. On their way, they had to pass through Wayanad. As they approached Wayanad, Arjun felt like he knew this place and he suddenly took control by instructing the driver where to go. The driver was confused, but Arjun insisted to take them where he wanted to go. Padmanabhan, his wife, Sandeep and Arjun were in the same vehicle along with one elderly person of the family. Padmanabhan asked the driver to follow where Arjun wanted to go. Arjun directed them inside a village, from there to a narrow lane, take some turns left and right and soon, they landed in front of the gates of a church. With lot of familiarity, Arjun got down, but he was still perplexed as to what had lead him there. He got down from the car, opened the gate of the church and started walking towards the main entrance.

Other family members in both the cars couldn't understand what was happening. They swiftly got down from the car and followed Arjun.

As Arjun was gradually walking towards the main door of the church, the gardener ran towards Arjun and asked him "Where were you all these days, Anthony baba? We all missed you."

Arjun couldn't say anything, but gently continued walking. On the way he turned towards the orphanage and walked towards it. The children saw Arjun approaching and in delight, all of them ran towards him! They held his hands lovingly, hugged him to express their love and asked, "Where were you Anthony? We simply couldn't bear being without you. We have already been abandoned by our parents. You are our parent, our God!! You please don't leave us. Our life is in your hands; don't let us lose everything again!!"

Arjun's parents were witnessing all this silently, but couldn't understand what was going on. By then, the message of Anthony's arrival had reached the pastor of the church and he rushed towards Anthony, crying "Anthony, my child! These kids were missing you all the time and have not even eaten anything in the last two days as a prayer offering for your return. They love you so much!!"

Arjun didn't speak a word. He was going through a personality split shock between Arjun and Anthony and trying to comprehend what was going on with his life. Arjun's parents stepped forward to talk to the pastor and take control of the situation. The noble pastor invited all of them inside his study-room nearby to discuss. Everyone followed him, including Arjun. The pastor courteously offered everyone a place to sit and some water to quench their thirst. He then narrated about the entire decade of a pious life that Anthony had spent in the church; his good deeds with the church; and his engagement with the children at the orphanage. In turn, Arjun's parents also narrated the first 20 years of Arjun's life and how they had lost him 10 years back and had suddenly gained him back few days back. They also expressed that having got Arjun, their son back, they would like him to be with them. The pastor understood the pain of the parents and let Arjun go.

Here, Arjun after hearing the last 10 years of his life from the pastor and experiencing the love of those children for him, was going through a mental dilemma.

Arjun asked the pastor: "Holy Father, tell me what should I do? Duty-bound as a son, my heart tells me that I should go with my parents, but knowing what I have been doing in the last 10 years, my heart also tells me that I have a larger duty towards these children and their future. Please resolve this confusion for me."

The pastor replies, "Arjun, my child, do what your heart contemplates is right. There is nothing right or wrong in choosing any one of your duty, as long as you are happy living with it. You should never look back in your life and regret the decision that you take now."

Arjun : "Father, one more thing that confuses me is, if I choose my duty towards the children, who will I be? A Christian- Anthony or a Hindu-Arjun?"

Pastor : "My child, who told you that religion, is determined by what your name is? Name is just an identification tag. It has nothing to do with the religion. You are a creation of your parents and your parents were just instrumental in creating you. The real creator is that formless divine presence which is present inside you, me and everyone. This creator is one and the same. We all are the creations of one creator and He doesn't differentiate between anybody. We have segregated this holistic divine creator for our own convenience, so that we can pray to a form and impose our faith towards that form. It is our own way of expressing our thanksgiving to our God and these man-made thanksgiving methods are called 'religion'. All our prayers ultimately culminate into that one single source and this source that we keep searching outside is nowhere but within each one of us. Bible says- Love thy neighbour as you love thyself. Quran says- If you have morsel of food and if your neighbour is starving, you do not belong to Islam. Jainism says- Live and let live. Hinduism says- One in All, All in One. Every religion conveys the same message in different forms that if you have to serve god, serve humanity. If that's the truth, then who are we to differentiate? Aren't Anthony and Arjun the same person from within in whatever you do?"

Arjun had a wave of clarity and he understood that his duty should be towards the larger interest. To seek God, he needed to serve the formless presence that exists in each and every one. He also understood that the abandoned children in the orphanage are the luckiest one, as they do not know their physical parent in this material world, but these children are associated to that universal parent, that formless gigantic force to guide them. If he as Arjun turns his back to these children, he is not fulfilling the purpose for which the Almighty must have sent him to this planet. It was to understand this truth that he had to go through such incidences in life so that he could find a meaning in his life, then connect back to his roots and later gain that wisdom to understand that life is larger than what we can perceive and understand.

Arjun told his parents that he had decided to stay back with the church and serve the children at the orphanage, but with a new name of Arjun. This was his way of showing respect towards his parents and committing himself to the service of god.

God upsets our plans, so that he can execute his plans for us through us. When God's plans are getting executed, surrender to His plans with happiness and know that his plans for us are always right.

Almighty has his own ways of awakening and handholding everyone to the mainstream life with a purpose. Understand this and live humble!!!

~~~ ~~~ ~~~

Chapter 9

Life of Purpose

This is a story of a beautiful, loving couple.

Varuna, a student of Paediatrics stream, had just cleared her graduation from the medical college, after which her father helped her in setting up her paediatric practice clinic. Varuna's father had always taught her the values of life, of how a person should have a purpose in life and how this purpose should be for the interest of the community and humanity. 'Any purpose that is for I, me and my family only creates a life lived for selfish reasons and human life is not something to be wasted only for material gains. Our life is God's gift unto us; how we live should be our gift unto him!!' were her father's teachings to Varuna. His lessons were ingrained in her thoughts and actions. She completely aligned herself to such noble thoughts.

Pradeep, a Mechanical engineer about two years elder to Varuna, stayed in the same residential complex where Varuna's parents had an apartment. Pradeep was brought up by his parents with utmost love and affection. They taught him the values of living life for the family and taking care of everyone in the family. They ingrained in him qualities of respect, politeness, humbleness and, above all, immense love for the family.

In his young age, Pradeep developed a liking for Varuna, but his polite nature and nervousness never allowed him to even speak to her, leave alone expressing his feelings to her. Whenever he saw Varuna, he held on to her with his eyes till she vanished from his sight. His actions and body language made his admiration for Varuna apparent to his friends as well as to Varuna. But Varuna did not approach Pradeep; she waited for him to initiate the first step.

This went on for nearly three years and the barrage of emotions couldn't be controlled anymore. One day, as Varuna was moving from her home to the nearby bus stand, it started raining and she wasn't carrying an umbrella with her. In an attempt to save herself from the rain, Varuna took shelter in a nearby shade of a shop just as Pradeep was moving out of the same shop after some grocery shopping. Seeing Varuna there, his joy knew no bounds! With utmost innocence and affection, Pradeep offered his umbrella to Varuna without realizing that he was getting drenched in the rain. This sight brought a smile on her face and that encouraged Pradeep to open up a conversation with Varuna. The initial talks were just introductory, comprising of basic questions, the answers to which they both seemed to know well! By then, the rain had stopped and Varuna started moving towards the bus stand. Pradeep gathered courage and asked if he could accompany her till the bus stand. Varuna replied in the positive. Both spent some more time together walking and talking affectionately till they reached the bus stand and then parted ways. Pradeep's happiness had reached cloud nine! He was in his own world with Varuna all around him, in his thoughts, in his mind, in his eyes, in his dreams and in his heart…

Next day, as Pradeep returned from his workplace in the evening, he happened to cross paths again with Varuna. This time he had no hesitation and directly approached her to chat. They talked casually for a few minutes and Varuna paused for a few seconds with expectation filled in her eyes as if she wanted Pradeep to say something. Pradeep could understand her feelings but couldn't muster courage to propose to her, due to the fear of rejection. Hesitatingly, Varuna handed over an envelope to Pradeep and started walking without glancing back. With nervousness, Pradeep opened the envelope only to find a black & white photograph of Varuna in it. It had her signature behind her photo with a single word "Yes" written over it. Pradeep realized that it was Varuna's reply to the question she anticipated from him which he didn't even have the courage to ask her. It was like heaven given to Pradeep without asking for it. Yes, they were in love, the beautiful expression that God has made all human beings with and that we as humans use so sparingly and selectively!!

The good human beings that Pradeep and Varuna were, they expressed their feelings about each other to their parents. Discussions went on within the family, as they were not of the same caste. Parents are those gate keepers who look into various artificial man-made boundaries to decide the happiness of their children, but love understands only one religion and one caste. Pradeep and Varuna could withstand all the concerns raised by their parents and finally made them agree and accept their relation. In no time, they were engaged to each other and even the date for their marriage was finalized. Their love was about to culminate into a happy ending, with a promise of a lovely new life of togetherness. Pradeep made a charming groom and Varuna made a beautiful bride at their wedding. The entire community and friends blessed this beautiful couple for a wonderful life of togetherness.

After a euphoric beginning, life turned usual for them in few days with Varuna handling her Paediatric clinic and Pradeep resuming back his job with a multi-national company.

Few months later, the entire family was thrilled with the news of Varuna expecting a baby. The entire family came together to welcome the bundle of joy's arrival in the family. Each one ensured to take utmost care of Varuna during her pregnancy. The expected grand-parents were the most eager ones – even more than Varuna and Pradeep.

Then, the day arrived when Varuna started experiencing labour pain and was rushed to hospital by her parents. Everyone in the family arrived at the hospital within an hour. In couple of hours the doctor broke the delightful news of the couple being blessed with a baby boy. Celebrations started at the hospital itself. Amidst all this, the doctor then asked Pradeep to meet him in person and left towards his cabin with Pradeep following him. After settling down in his chair within his cabin, the doctor asked Pradeep to ensure that the doors of his cabin were closed properly. Then, the doctor communicated to Pradeep in strict confidence his concern. The information shook Pradeep by his roots!!!

Doctor : "Let me tell you that in medical history such instances occur and I have seen few such cases, but it is my duty to share with you my observation, so that you can prepare yourself and the family for any eventuality. When the child was born, he didn't cry. We checked his heartbeat, pulse and found everything normal, but he didn't cry initially even after a few taps on his back. Later, he cried but it was not normal and he suddenly was silent again. This is not a normal sign and hence I thought of sounding it to you. The child is now normal but as parents, you need to observe him. At a convenient time, later but within next few days, communicate this to Varuna. I am sure she being a paediatrician herself, will understand the situation better."

Pradeep was speechless. He didn't know how to respond to what he had just heard. Should he celebrate this moment of joy or start preparing for something which he was not even aware of as to how it will manifest in his life?!

Pradeep decided to keep this information to himself, till an appropriate time to share it with Varuna, came forth. In few days' time, Varuna was discharged from the hospital and the family happily came back with the new-born into their house. For Varuna, she had to bring up her son with lots of values in life and for Pradeep, the concern and prayer was that the child should be healthy and alright. Within couple of weeks, Varuna started expressing to Pradeep that she felt a bit concerned with the child's behaviour, as he was neither drinking milk properly nor was he responding to any movement of simple toys that babies normally respond to. Pradeep realized that it was now time to share with Varuna the concerns that doctor had expressed.

After Pradeep divulged all the information to Varuna, she was in tears. Her eyes were soaked with deep emotional pain. Pradeep could only try his best to console her and convince her to accept the child the way he was.

Being a courageous lady and a concerned mother, Varuna accumulated courage and decided to get her child diagnosed from a Neonatologist. The child was put through a few tests. They also took the second opinion of an expert to be doubly sure of the state of the child. Finally the doctors communicated to Varuna and Pradeep that they feared the child to be autistic. Learning this, the parents were torn apart and their care and concern for the child multiplied manifolds to insulate him from the outer world.

(Autism is a developmental disability. These are disorders that occur at some stage in a child's development, often retarding the development. On an average 1 in every 5000 children in India, is autistic. The magnitude and severity of autism varies from case-to-case.)

Once again Varuna stood up bravely to face the situation in front of them. She started gathering more information about autism and its related treatments. She took a bold step of deciding not to continue with her paediatric practice and instead, stay at home to take care of her child. They had named the child 'Ansh', meaning 'an integral part of us'!!

Varuna's curiosity to know more about autism led her to understand that there are many children like Ansh who are autistic and they are not treated well in the society nor is there an acceptance for them. The society has sympathy towards such children but does not give them a place of respect. This disturbed Varuna deeply. Being a noble person, she didn't think only about herself and her child, but her thoughts were inclusive in nature. Her father's teachings, blessing and values made her more determined at a time of such anguish. She started wondering how she could help change this scenario to help such children gain societal respect, as also, help the parents of autistic children to deal with the situation in a more matured manner and start accepting the fact that their child needs special care and attention.

Varuna shared her thoughts with Pradeep. Pradeep was always supportive of Varuna and in these thoughts, he also found a noble cause. So, he volunteered to support her. Varuna began her work by communicating about her goal to some of her known friends and doctors. Through them, she got to know about six more children who were also diagnosed autistic. She approached their parents and volunteered to take care of their children in a day-care module where she would help them learn how to differentiate things and how to read alphabets. The parents agreed and Varuna started her day-care centre for these children at her home itself. Along with these six children, Varuna also took care of Ansh and ensured that she gave utmost care and importance to every child.

News of Varuna's noble venture soon spread around through word-of-mouth. Within six months, there were other parents approaching Varuna to help their autistic child get a more meaningful learning and living. Varuna realized that this path was giving her a meaningful purpose and she could make a significant positive difference to the community by supporting the cause of autistic children. However, lack of adequate space and the requirement of additional persons to handle more number of children, were proving to be hindrances.

Varuna's relentless pursuit helped her overcome all the concerns that came her way. Through her resolute aspiration, Varuna soon realised her dream of starting a facility where she could take care of 250 such children, equipped with the requisite infrastructure to support this noble cause. It is said that when we start believing in something intensely, the whole universe conspires to make it happen for us. For Varuna, this turned out to be a reality, as her faith and belief in her cause was beyond the limits of passion, nurtured with utmost compassion.

As it happened, one autistic child's parents had a huge apartment on the ground floor which was an ideal location to accommodate easily 60-70 children.

They volunteered to give their apartment for free usage to Varuna so that she could operate her centre for autistic children care, from there. There were few other parents who volunteered to spend couple of hours with the children coming to this centre and it made sense to have them on board as volunteers as such parents could handle the children with empathy and care. Varuna had to just nod her head in favour to get the things rolling and her God was with her in her journey of holding the hands of autistic children and bringing them into the mainstream of life!!!

Today, Ansh is 10 years old and what started with Ansh is now an institution of 150 autistic children operating out of three centres. Varuna's working with passion for her purpose in life has elevated her from a being mother to Ansh to a mother of 150 autistic children who look forward to a guide in their life. The Centre has a set of 15 trained teachers to handle autistic children and their focus is to spread happiness in the life of the children, as well as, make their parents live a life of happiness with the special child that God has blessed them with.

Almighty has his own ways of awakening and handholding everyone towards finding a purpose in life!!!

Chapter 10

Ingrained Values

Madhav was an aspirational salesman in an electrical company that sold audio & video systems to schools and colleges. The Company sold a package of product and after-sales service to its customers. Madhav was in-charge of Delhi state and was one of the top three sales representatives of the company. Ramprasad was another sales representative based out of Bangalore, selling same products to the clients in the state of Karnataka. Every three months when the sales performance of the company would be reviewed, these two names would always feature in the top three salespersons' list. There was a stiff competition between both of them to out-beat each other. However, their Sales Manager knew very well that both of them could not be compared. Madhav was a sweet talker whose ability was in converting calls to customers and getting repeat service orders that ensured his billing targets. Whereas, Ramprasad was thorough with his product knowledge and could sell the product based on its differentiating factors and uninterrupted support & servicing, resulting in more product sales. Hence, both their capabilities were different and their manager always looked for a blend of both to make the best salesman combination model to replicate across the country.

However, the fact is that, while all are born equals in potential, it is differential performance that helps performers emerge from among the mediocre.

In every quarterly review meeting, Madhav and Ramprasad would meet and discuss how they could learn from each other to grow more in their respective careers. Madhav would always discuss like an entrepreneur and also express his aspiration towards crossing the learning curve fast with an intent of starting his own company selling similar products with the kind of clientele he had developed and the market knowledge he had gained over the years. Ramprasad would get attracted to such thoughts, but his risk-taking ability was much lower as compared to Madhav. However the seed of entrepreneurship within Ramprasad was already sowed by Madhav through his thoughts and plans. After many such sessions of discussions over nearly two years, once Madhav communicated to Ramprasad that all his plans and financials were in place and in a span of three months, he would be letting go this job to start his own venture and test his luck in business. He also asked Ramprasad if he was willing to join him as a partner. Madhav had a lucrative offer to make, whereby Ramprasad did not have to invest any money and yet get to directly handle the South and West market of the country with a profit-sharing model of 25%. Ramprasad started counting sleepless nights after such an offer. He knew that Madhav's zeal could certainly make this new venture start, grow and sustain. If he joined hands with Madhav, Ramprasad would also get an opportunity to do something for his own and grow from there. After a few days of thinking, finally Ramprasad decides to plunge into business with Madhav. Both of them resign from the services of the company.

On an auspicious day, Madhav and Ramprasad inaugurate their company and commence contacting prospective clients. As their area of operation is well-defined, with Madhav handling north plus east and Ramprasad handling south plus west, there was no scope for any personality clash. Even within the other aspects of the business, Madhav took charge of administration and finance, and Ramprasad handled the field team's training and development needs. The business progressed and in a span of three years they were earning more money than what they were earning as salary from their earlier company. They had achieved freedom from all kinds of financial burden and had to now only focus on scaling the business to greater heights, expanding their team and participating more in designing strategic roadmaps for their young thriving business.

Analysis and review of financials and various segments of revenue were important to ensure they are progressively growing and making reasonable profits in the product and services. During one such review discussion between Madhav and Ramprasad, Ramprasad observed that there was a substantial revenue generation on sale of spare parts and accessories from north and east with very low cost and that was contributing a good amount to the profits. He couldn't understand the entire revenue segment and hence inquired with Madhav as to what revenue model is it that he wasn't aware of and why was it not operated in his area of south plus west? In response, Madhav just asked Ramprasad to ignore the same and focus on the profitability in his designated areas. However, Ramprasad's curiosity did not allow him to rest and hence he insisted that he should also be informed about any such revenue model. If it was implementable, he didn't see any reason why they could not implement it in south plus west as well. Madhav mistook this as an additional revenue opportunity and agreed to share it with Ramprasad in strict confidence.

Madhav: "I have designed an inspection mechanism wherein, after the completion of one year of sale of the audio & video system to the corporates or the educational institute, I personally go to inspect and take a complete access of the system. During this inspection, without anyone noticing, I cut a wire of the system and loosely connect it again, so that the system is still functional. I then communicate it to their facility manager that we have inspected the system and it is functionally ok, but there are certain parts which have waned out and shall need replacement. The client can continue using the system till it stops working and whenever it stops, they should let us know, so that we can get the spare part/ accessories replaced. As I know the wire is loose, it normally gets disconnected in a couple of days and I get a call from the client. I go there with some spare parts in my bag and act as if I am replacing some worn-out parts and bill them for such spare parts. Through this smart move I have grown the billing for spares without any input cost and at the same time, the client also feels happy that I have sounded them well in advance and have taken care of their problem in time."

Ramprasad was shocked to hear this, as this was completely against his value system. He did not know how to respond to what he had just heard from Madhav. For Ramprasad, this was equivalent to cheating. He felt that it was no less than an atrocious act of looting the customers; something that he couldn't even dream of. This episode led to an argument between Ramprasad and Madhav, resulting in serious difference of opinion. It led to such a level that both decide to split their ways, as the basic value systems were at stake and Ramprasad was not prepared to associate himself with any such business whose roots were ingrained towards cheating the customers.

Ramprasad decided to start on his own with whatever he had. He was bent on doing a business that is ethical and customer-focused towards better products and service. Ramprasad was not prepared to be a part of any growth that came with compromise.

Years passed by. Madhav continued his business in his way and Ramprasad ventured into a new business with his values and principles. Once, Ramprasad heard that Madhav had contracted some serious illness. In spite of the difference in their value-systems, Ramprasad couldn't let go of his emotional attachment for Madhav and travelled from Bangalore to Delhi to meet Madhav at the hospital. Madhav had suffered and survived a heart attack and held deep regret within himself. Ramprasad spent some time with Madhav at the hospital and as a good friend, advised him not to indulge in wrong practices but rather make his life useful for others, thereby creating value for the society and self. Madhav somehow agreed to all that Ramprasad said, least at that moment. Feeling relieved that his friend shall now walk a path of values and good principles, Ramprasad came back to his hometown in Bangalore and continued his business.

After a couple of years, Ramprasad once again happened to meet Madhav during a seminar in Mumbai. Both the friends chatted for some time and decided to meet in the evening for dinner together. They met at a restaurant as decided and started inquiring about each other, their health, family and various other aspects of life. Later Ramprasad was curious to know what Madhav was doing now for his living. Hence, the inquiry now moved towards that direction.

Ramprasad : "Tell me my friend, what you do now? Are you still continuing the same business or did you finally change path to do something good for self and the society?"

Madhav : "After that incident, I changed myself completely. I sold off that business and made some good money. I had to do something to keep my entrepreneurship flowing, as well as, to sustain my earning. I then designed a new business model, conceived the thought and implemented it. This new business doesn't give me that much money, but I earn enough to take care of my needs. The money I had earned by selling the earlier business is earning me good interest in addition to the profits from the current business. I am happy with that much."

Ramprasad (with inquisitiveness) : "But what's this new business model? Can you share some details of it?"

Madhav (proudly) : Yes, sure. As I knew most of the clients in the space of education institutions and corporates, I designed my new business around these clients only. I, through my new company called "MSRe Pvt Ltd", approached them to buy their old furniture. This entire business of buying is handled by a Purchase Manager who manages this company and controls the inventory of such old furniture purchased. This furniture is then sent in for refurbishing and made to look like new. All the new looking furniture is then sold by MSRe to my other company named "OF-DeN Pvt Ltd". OF-DeN keeps an inventory of such furniture. Whenever my clients require new furniture, I sell them this refurbished furniture as new and make a decent profit of 50 to 75%."

Ramprasad, stunned with what he had just heard, asked, "Does that also mean rotating old with new and also selling to same client the old as new without their knowledge?"

Madhav confirmed it by nodding his head in affirmative.

Ramprasad couldn't hold on the confused anger within him and said: "You have not changed a bit, Madhav. Earlier you were directly cheating your client. Now you have simply inserted an intermediary step called refurbishing, in your scheme of things. If that refurbishing part is taken out, you are still in the business of cheating your clients!!! How is your conscience allowing you to do this?"

Unfazed, Madhav replied : The name of my company is explicit enough. If the clients do not inquire, it's their fault; not mine."

Ramprasad asked in curiosity : "And can you please explain me how is that?"

Madhav : "MSRe" is "Madhav Scraps & Refurbishing" and "OF-DeN" is "Old Furniture Designed New".

Hearing this, Ramprasad could not hold his laughter!

Later that night as Ramprasad was returning to his hotel, his mind was still analysing the entire episode for a deeper understanding. He realized that it was all about the value systems that a person believes in and he has all the justifications to prove his point right, irrespective of how others think about him or his thoughts. Such thought processes deeply ingrained become the person's personality and character. As said by Clement Stone "The mind of the man is the man.

Change the mind and we can change the man". If the mind has ingrained such values and has firm belief in it, no one can change it. A change is only possible if the person himself determines to change it. Nobody can influence or infuse a change. As said by Henry Ford " You believe you can, you believe you can't, either way you are right".

These thoughts led to a greater revelation that there are no good/right thoughts or bad/wrong thoughts, there are only thoughts and in "My World", my thoughts are always good and right, irrespective of what "The World" thinks of it!!!

Chapter 11

The Power of Gratitude

Sharat was a successful businessman, running a business empire worth $250 million. Sharat was a well reputed personality in the industry. Sharat had built his entire business from the scratch, through sheer hard work and determination. He had started his career as an employee with a company, learned the ropes of business in no time, understood about the optimum utilization of resources in the right manner and always showed due respect to all people. Needless to say, these attributes made him immensely popular. Fuelled by these qualities and his innate desire to start his own business, coupled by his strong belief in himself, had led Sharat to start and build an empire in barely two decades.

All was going exceedingly well for Sharat. The desire for further growth led him towards a takeover deal that he struck for a whopping sum of $100 million with an expectation of increased revenue of $50 million per year. All due-diligence was in place, every financial and strategic evaluation was successfully carried out. The business deal was executed smoothly and Sharat gained complete management control over the company that he had taken over. The initial days went off well according to plan. However, problems started surfacing just six months later, where few realizations shook Sharat like the horrifying waves of a tsunami that hit the shore unawares!! The valuations of the new business that was taken over proved totally wrong. It turned out that there were huge contingent liabilities towards certain disputes with the tax department that were never reported nor informed. Also, there were pending workers' settlement with an impact of arrears payable for past three years. This too was hidden during the evaluation, with the result that after the take-over the workers went on strike.

Sharat was at an utter loss about how to handle these two sudden shockers that had huge financial implications on him. They not only took away the expected gains from this business, but were also sucking into the funds of his existing and thriving business. Sharat wanted an immediate solution to these issues. During this challenging phase, he came across a young dynamic professional named Divian, who was polite and had a positive attitude towards life. Divian could see a solution for any problem and in Sharat's problems too, he suggested some recourse to him. Sharat was impressed by the thoughts of this young man and was ready to bet on him, as Divian made it clear that he needs only time to resolve the issue and not money, which made sense for Sharat. They agreed on a time-frame of 60 days and Sharat gave Divian complete freedom and authority during this time frame. Sharat assured Divian that he would back Divian for any action that shall be taken by him during this period. With this assurance, Divian went ahead with his action plan.

Divian approached the tax department and explained them the status of the new management. He urged them that they should not be harsh on the new management on account of the old cases and that, they should give a deferment facility to the new management, so that they could get a breather to earn profits from this business and pay the old dues out of such money generated from this business itself. He explained to the tax authorities that if this was not permitted, then Sharat's business house would have no option than to let go this business and sell it to some new business group who may not be able to do justice to the industry. Add to that, the loss from this deal would be claimed as expense by the existing investor to get a huge tax benefit. Hence, in the benefit of all, Divian requested the tax authorities to accept his proposal, as Sharat held a lot of advantage to his employees, the corporate sector, to the tax department, to the industry, as well as to the country for generating more business. The tax authorities saw sense in what Divian had proposed and sought time to get this restructuring proposal concurred by the Chief Minister of the state, as it was a unique proposal and thus wasn't within their ambit of the authorities. Divian agreed and requested them to issue such an order within 45 days, else Sharat's corporation would pull out their investment from this group.

Next, Divian approached the workers' union and understood their grievances. Knowing that they had not been paid increments for past three years, Divian made an upfront commitment of 15% increment per annum to a total of 45% for 3 years put together. This shocked the workers' union as they never felt someone would come and accept their demand and rather, offer them even more than what they expected without any negotiations. After this, Divian took control over the meeting and made some bold statements that left the members of the union spellbound. Divian communicated that while the new management had all the intention to pay the increments as they believed that profits should be shared with the workers; the fact was that there were no profits as of now! Hence, the need of the hour was for everyone to trust the new management and start working efficiently as a team, so as to help meet the organisation's goals for profits to be generated efficiently and effectively. The profits would, in turn, be paid back as increments to the team in two forms, half of it as one-time payment and the balance half of it over next 12 months. The workers found this option interesting, especially as it depicted more of participation, involvement and togetherness. They wilfully accepted the proposal, called off the strike and began their work.

Divian became a star in the organization overnight, with every employee feeling a connect with him. In him, they saw a leader who had passion and compassion towards organisation's goals as well as for people's interest. Sharat was relaxed as he had found a new leader who could shoulder his responsibilities and support his business. The business started growing and improving under the joint leadership of Sharat and Divian, more so due to Divian, because the employees connected very well with him.

Sharat's son, Jagdish had just stepped into the family business and Sharat felt it appropriate to train him under the able leadership of Divian. In no time, Jagdish turned out to be an immense admirer of Divian and would always praise Divian before Sharat. Over time, what happened was that even though Sharat held admiration for Divian, he now started feeling a sense of insecurity as he felt Jagdish would land up under Divian's leadership and may risk the enterprise that Sharat had built up. Further more, Sharat was in for a bigger shocker when he realized that his daughter Radhika held deep feelings for

Divian! She perceived it as love and had started dreaming of a married life with Divian. Sharat's emotions could not handle all this, as, for him, Divian was his creation and today, he stood to lose everything he had created due to his own protégé. The idea was too intense for Sharat to bear.

Thus, Sharat started conspiring to eliminate Divian out of the way. He pooled together few of his well-wishers and plotted to trap Divian in some misdoing that would let him down amongst all his loved ones, and thus help Sharat regain everything that was rightfully his own. However, Divian was so strong of character that all of Sharat's evil plans failed. Instead, Divian gained more popularity and credibility in the eyes of others. People also could see that Divian had immense gratitude towards Sharat for everything in his life and hence he held no iota of doubt that Sharat was behind all these misdeeds..

However, the turn of events made Sharat even more restless. His anger turned to distress and he increasingly kept craving for revenge on Divian. Sharat's self-created monster of insecurity grew so large that he started fearing that Divian would take everything away from him. In this angst, Sharat thought of something very cruel - that was to get Divian eliminated. For this, Sharat needed someone trustworthy to help him find a professional killer who would act upon money to kill Divian. In strict confidence, Sharat shared this with Jagdish who was shocked to know this, but later Jagdish understood from his father that if Jagdish didn't support Sharat, he would find someone else to help him out. Also, Sharat was very clear in his mind that he was doing all this for Jagdish's future only. Finally, Jagdish agreed to help his father identify such a person, knowing very well that his father was determined and no sense could prevail on him now.

However, filled with despair about what his father was doing, Jagdish also worked out another plan. He decided to take Divian into confidence and tell him about his father's conspiracy, to help Divian get out of it in time. On hearing what Jagdish had to say, Divian was perplexed. He never knew that the person who he had looked up to in life, would conspire so badly against him. He never thought that Sharat would hold such terrible animosity against him that he would decide to murder him. Divian was equally surprised that Jagdish had shared all this with him and inquired as to why he did so? To this, Jagdish responded that he wanted to save his father from doing something grossly wrong and at the same time, he wanted to save life of his mentor whom he looked up to immensely. Also he revealed to Divian that his sister Radhika was in love with Divian and he didn't want her to suffer in any way.

For Divian, the entire world had suddenly taken a reverse rotation, as Sharat whom he looked up to for so many years, had suddenly come across as his biggest enemy; Jagdish, with whom he had just a working relation, turned out to be his biggest admirer and life saver; and Radhika, the owner's daughter, who for him was just a relation of respect, was someone wanting to live a life together with him. He didn't know how to handle this upside down life-scenario presented to him; but he knew that he had to face it!. Both Divian and Jagdish wanted a solution to handle this situation. They jointly agreed that Divian should leave the city that same night and settle in some other far-off place. Jagdish would help with sufficient funds to suffice Divian for two years at least. They also decided that Divian would never return to the city and would keep his identity secret. This was for the interest of Divian and hence, he wilfully agreed, but yet, the question foremost on his mind remained unanswered. That question was, how could Sharat think like this about Divian and treat him as an arch enemy, dangerous enough to be eliminated?

As decided, that night Divian did a vanishing act. No one in the company knew about it, except Abhay, a close associate of Divian who helped him with all the arrangements and helped search for a safe place where he could move without getting identified by anyone. Divian's safety for next few days was the responsibility of Abhay under the close guidance of Jagdish, as he had complete information of what Sharat's plans were from time to time. All this went on for next two months till Sharat was assured that Divian was no more traceable and thus, no more a threat. Sharat breathed a sigh of relief and took control over the business. But, the soul of the business was missing as Divian was no more in the company and the employees had lost their leader whom they looked up to!!! The setbacks of this were felt across the company and over a period of next two years, the organisation faced major challenges time and again. By this time Sharat had settled himself well in life and got both his children Jagdish and Radhika married. They too had settled in their own lives, with Radhika moving to another city with her husband and Jagdish participating in Sharat's business as his successor.

Meanwhile, at a distant place, Divian was on survival mode earning to live. However his intrinsic drive towards business didn't let him relax for long. He conceptualized a business model and initiated a process to execute the same. Divian ensured that his business model would in no way clash with that of Sharat, as he never intended to be a competition to someone who he respected and looked up to. Divian rolled out his business model in a small way but his intentions and strategies were so well in place that the success was beyond anticipation and he couldn't handle it alone. Divian was in need of good trustworthy persons to grow his business. He thought of Abhay and tried to establish contact with him. On connecting with Abhay, Divian realized that Abhay had already left Sharat's company and so had many others! They were also ready to join Divian in any of his entrepreneurial venture, as they had firm belief in Divian!! This was a message of relief for Divian and he immediately started putting his actions together to expand his organization and find suitable positions for 25 such people who he could trust in the journey of expanding his business. With the collective force of rejuvenated intelligence, the new business flourished and started showing excellent results. Soon, Divian's success was spoken about widely in the industry and even Sharat and Jagdish couldn't remain uninformed of this success story.

Sharat got wild with the thought of Divian's success, especially knowing that all his earlier employees were with Divian in his success!!! Sharat's mind went back to the old thoughts of eliminating Divian. In this process, he discovers that the city where Divian has headquartered his business, is where Radhika and her husband stay. As Radhika's husband is also in business, Sharat masterminds a plan engaging his son-in-law. He plans to ask Radhika's husband to fix up a meeting with Divian over dinner at a restaurant on a pretext of a business deal and to take over Divian by shock, through his goons and then murder Divian to get rid of him forever.

As planned, Radhika's husband who is unaware of Sharat's malicious interest, invites Divian for a meeting; Divian accepts the invite. Radhika's husband arrives at the hotel; however, due to heavy rains, Divian cannot make it for the meeting. Due to network problems, he also cannot call up Radhika's husband to inform about the change in plans. Radhika's husband waits for long and in disgust, enters the restaurant for a cup of coffee. As he settles down himself, an unknown person approaches him and just inquires "Divian?" Not knowing what he means, Radhika's husband responds " Yes!!" in the next few moments pass in a blur. In a fraction of a second, the man pulls out his gun and shoots Radhika's husband down. He breaths his last on the table itself!!

Later that day, Sharat gets to know what happened, and gets immensely scared. He makes plans to escape from the city immediately. However, he cannot hide from the law for long and gets caught by the police after barely three months. Sharat's conspiracy to kill Divian gets revealed. However, Divian rushes to the police station with his lawyer to release Sharat under bail. Sharat feels extremely ashamed of himself when he sees that Divian is the only one to come forward to protect him at this time. In that annoying moment, Sharat asks Divian: "I have always hated you and even decided to kill you, but how come you have always been so good to me?"

Divian smiles and replies: "Whose life were you trying to take away? My life itself is a gift of yours. I always did everything and anything to please you and to win your trust. My life was meant for you. I always looked up to you as an inspiration and was always indebted in deepest gratitude to you. It didn't matter how you perceived me, but for me, you were the source of faith and I always drew energy and life through you. You have been everything for me and I continue to believe so."

Sharat was shocked to hear these words. He didn't know how to respond and was in deep misery of having misunderstood Divian for long and having unnecessarily given birth to an internal enemy for no reason. In pain, Sharat said to Divian, "ask whatever you want from me and I shall grant you the same. Today I do not see you as an enemy, but as an extension of myself."

Divian, humbly with folded hands spoke "If so, then if you see me as a person of worth, please give your daughter Radhika to me as my wife and take me into your company so that I can serve and support you and Jagdish in growing your organisation"

Divian's words filled Sharat's eyes with tears of repent and joy of salvation. Not only did Divian propose to give a new life to his widowed daughter, but also accepted Jagdish as the next successor for the organisation with a commitment to serve the organization for its growth.

Sharat, in turn, accepted Divian as the head of the family with Radhika's responsibility and Jagdish's well-being to be decided by Divian and Divian reciprocated by fulfilling his words to his master till his last breath.

Gratitude has miraculous powers of turning every circumstance to acceptance with humility!!!

~~ ~~ ~~

Chapter 12

Celebration & Respect

Ashok, a supply chain professional was employed with a reputed organization in the department of distribution and logistics. However, he was not happy working at this place because his potential was not getting utilized to the optimum and hence he was getting increasingly frustrated. Ashok was seeking an opening outside in the organisation where he felt he could explore himself and his potential to its best. Then, one day, Ashok was contacted for a suitable opening in a new start-up organization and he willingly accepted it. The offer was from Carryon. com, a company in the business of on-line ordering and despatches. Ashok was thrilled with the offer, as he had lots to explore and do to fulfil his professional desires and aspirations. He cleared the interview and was offered the role of Head-Supply Chain Management. Even before joining the company, Ashok was in a great mood for celebration. After receiving the offer, the first thing he did was to take his family out for dinner and celebrate with them the new role that he was so thrilled about. He spoke to his friends about the new job and the new company with a lot of zeal and told them whatever he knew about the company which, incidentally, was yet to be set up. There was lots of happiness and celebration in his voice when he spoke about the new organization.

Then the day arrived when Ashok was to join the company. He selected his best dress for that day and ensured that he reached the new office before time. With a bit of nervousness, he stepped inside the office with prayers on his lips, seeking the blessings of the Lord in making his journey in this organisation a success. As he was early, he was the first to reach and had to wait at the reception for 20 minutes. Later, the Executive Assistant (EA) to the CEO arrived and seeing that Ashok was waiting, greeted him with respect and led him to his new office. The EA made Ashok feel comfortable by offering him some refreshments and some initial reading materials about the company. Once the CEO reached his office, the EA invited Ashok to the CEO's cabin. As Ashok entered the cabin, he observed the CEO was preparing himself to welcome him. They exchanged greetings and the CEO offered Ashok some tea and then got into knowing each of them a little more in detail. The intention was to make Ashok feel comfortable and relaxed before he was explained about his job profile.

Later, the CEO handed over the synopsis of a strategic plan document to Ashok to go through and understand the company's philosophy, vision, mission and its strategic plans. Ashok was then introduced to the other team members. He noticed that the entire office was empty and in total there were only five members in the office. Apart from the two who he had already met, there was a Marketing Manager and an IT Manager. When Ashok broached his concern about such a small team with the CEO, he was informed that as it was a start-up company, recruitments were still on and the key critical positions are taken on priority. Ashok was the fifth person to be recruited. He was told that interviews were on for the rest of the positions and the candidates would be finalized within next two months' time. The CEO also told Ashok that "even though we all have a primary role to play, we need to ensure that till the entire team is in place we should be flexible enough to do whatever is required to keep the organization's work going on without any hindrances". Ashok was thrilled, as he was a person who believed in doing anything and everything in his career and here, he was being given such a fabulous opportunity that he would never miss.

The next few months in Ashok's life brought about long working hours and doing multiple things, from setting up the company, designing the interiors, getting the interior work done, negotiating with vendors for purchase of capital assets for business start-up, working on strategy plan for finding the sourcing partners, working on finding solutions to reach the goods to the customers without any delay, identifying stocking positions to keep the minimum inventory required at minimal cost, supporting the CEO in designing the organization's operational structure, helping HR draft the company policies, supporting Finance in setting up the computer systems and selection of software for financial data integrity.... The list never seemed to end! Name a job and Ashok was there as the trusted commander to execute the precise need of the organization.

There was hardly any time for Ashok to spare for himself in all these daily chores of the initial phase of setting up and he too never bothered about it. He also completely ignored his near & dear ones as he never wanted to be deviated from his focus on "the day of the company's inauguration". Now Ashok's day started at 8 am and ended at 11 pm, seven days a week. But, he still garnered energy to pull on – never wanting to miss any deadline as the launch of the Company was already announced and there was lot more to do. The CEO had given him complete responsibility to complete many of the aspects and Ashok never wanted any such thing to happen that would break the CEO's trust in him.

Finally, the day of the company's official inauguration arrived. The entire team was in place. The headcount of the company now was 42 and Ashok was a key instrumental person within the organization. Even on the inaugural day, when everyone were celebrating, Ashok was still with the IT Consultant working on the final trials and testing of the billing module to ensure that the inventory reporting and revenue accounting was properly captured in the system. The next day morning the first invoice was to be booked and Ashok never wanted an iota of error in the inaugural transaction of business. The next day, the "muhurat" (auspicious) invoicing was done in the presence of Board of Directors and CEO and it was successfully executed. The Company had achieved its first milestone of initial commencement. Ashok's selfless approach and commitment was acknowledged and appreciated and he felt happy about it.

Now, since the business had commenced, the functional roles had to be redefined, as the company could have no longer operated like before as one single team with no particular hierarchy and anybody taking up any job he/she liked. In the rejig process, Ashok got the role of Distribution and Logistics for which he was initially appointed. Considering his commitment levels, Ashok was also given the responsibility of Procurement and IT. This motivated Ashok, as he felt his hard work was being rightfully recognized and encouraged.

Since he was working continuously along side the CEO, Ashok developed a close association with him.

His focus towards work made him believe that life was all about work and only work. Somewhere, he ignored the human aspect and in this casualness, he would challenge any person within the organization when he felt things were not right in terms of benefit to the organization. Most of the times, the CEO supported Ashok, but occasionally he also gave him the feedback that sometimes Ashok needed to overlook the absence of perfection and understand the humane aspect, as it would help Ashok in building good relations with people and thereby motivate them to work to achieve near-perfect results.

However, Ashok never followed this, as for him relations were not the priority; for him, work and its perfect execution were the only things that mattered. So engrossed was Ashok in his inflexibility towards work that, without realizing, he had burned relations with some of his colleagues in an attempt to get the work right. Ashok didn't focus on developing relations and due to this, his language with his team and colleagues was little to do with respect and comprised more of instructions. Slowly, acceptance for Ashok within the other employees of the company started going down drastically. As Ashok had a critical role to play and his deliverables were also above expectations, he was a vital member of the team but with such a behaviour, it became challenging for his teammates to work with him. His team gradually started disengaging and leaving the organization one after the other.

Strangely, whenever an employee would put in his papers, Ashok's demeanour towards him/her would change unbelievably. He would express appreciation and gratitude towards that person during their last few working days with the organization. He would only talk good about such a colleague and would wholeheartedly share the contributions made by the person. During the farewell of that teammate, Ashok would get emotional and would be the one talking all good about the person. Ashok always spoke with respect about the person who had left the company and never uttered a single negative word against him/her. This behaviour surprised others, as they realized that Ashok was a hard task master who would only focus on work and would fail to appreciate the person when he/she was around. However, they realised that, even though he never appreciated it, Ashok would keenly notice and respect the person's good work but would become vocal about it only after the person left the organisation.

Finally, this feedback was shared with Ashok. He realized the grave mistake he was committing, which in turn was leading to excellent employees leaving the company. Ashok committed himself to improve upon this aspect and ensured that he forged good relations with his colleagues and teammates. To a large extent, Ashok succeeded in bringing that change within him.

Resultantly, the Company did exceedingly well and operated for ten years. Ashok progressed with the company and also built an excellent rapport with his team and stake holders. Resultant, Ashok was promoted and made Head of the Organisation.

Due to some strategic and structural changes in the business model, the Board of Directors decided to wind up the company and Ashok was instructed to carry out the winding up process. In fact, he was instructed to complete the entire process. He had to submit an action plan for the company closure and employee account settlement. Ashok did his best to put forth an action plan to ensure that every employee was taken care of properly and that the transition period was smooth for each and every employee. He also spoke to several recruitment agencies to outplace some of his employees and saw if he could negotiate an agreeable retrenchment package for the rest. His intention was to ensure that every employee's house was protected and they continued to have their daily earning till they found and settled in a new job.

Ashok treated every employee with respect. This was the first time that in such an instance he only thought about the individual employees and expressed his concern for each one of them. Every employee was treated with high dignity and respect. In six months' time, the entire process was completed and it was now time for Ashok to leave the company. He too left remembering all that he had gone through over the last ten years, recollecting all the good moments he spent with each and every employee or rather, his friends as he now called them. Whether they remembered him or not, Ashok recollected the wonderful time spent with each one of them during the best as well as the worst days of the company. Every memory was filled with lots of celebration and respect. He also counted the mistakes he had committed on account of his immature behaviour while handling relations and how he repented for that later. He went through the memory lane and realized that it was not worth spending a mechanical life at the cost of human relations!!

This led him to realize the biggest serene secret of Life, which God revealed it to him through this experience. Ashok realized that in life,

When we are born, there is CELEBRATION all around and anyone and everyone associated to us is happy of our arrival.

When we are dead and gone, everyone speaks with RESPECT about us, remembers us for may be few days or few years and then forget us.

Hence, life begins with celebration and ends with respect. This is true for everybody. What is most imperative is not what happens at the beginning or at the end, but the life that we live in between this journey of celebration and respect i.e. between birth and death. We need to understand that this gap is also filled with celebration and respect. If we can do so, then in real sense we have lived our life with fulfilment, understanding the eternal truth that our life is a gift of God to us and how we live should be our gift to God. Life is not about struggle but living in harmony with other human beings, finding reasons for celebration and respecting every human being with gratitude. Such a life lived is full of love, bliss, harmony, peace and celebration.

~~~ ~~~ ~~~

Chapter 13

Time & Space

Rajeev, was an enthusiastic IT professional just in the beginning of his career. As a youngster, he had a lot to get distracted with, due to his circle of influence through his close friends. As he was staying in a hostel away from his family, he had all the free time in the evening to loiter around and he even didn't bother to utilize it in right ways for self-development. Rajeev took his life very casually and spent days as they came by and blew up every bit of money he earned on parties, friends and gadgets.

Rajeev was introduced to gambling by one of his friends and he willingly indulged into the same. The habit got to him so much that he borrowed money to merely satisfy his desire of exploring gambling techniques and lost heavily in his exploration. This led him to a situation of unrest and desperation, with many of his friends following up for getting their money back which Rajiv had borrowed from them. Rajeev couldn't handle this mental trauma and lost all control of his life. Soon, he started thinking that if his life was not in his control, then he had no reason to live. Thus, he finally decided to commit suicide to escape from his mounting problems.

Rajeev wanted to be sure that his attempt should result into a fatal end, for he could no more live miserably. Rajeev had a final party with all his friends with his mind clearly knowing this was his last meeting with them, Hence, he was very careful dealing with them and was very loving with all of them for the whole evening. The next evening, he moved towards a nearby mountain cliff to execute his plan. It was an isolated place and Rajeev was sure that a jump off the cliff would end all his troubles. He reached there by twilight and waited for sunset, as he wanted to enjoy the scenic beauty of sun getting swallowed by the semi-circled orbit where sea meets and the sea slowly swallowing the ball of fire. He could somehow see a resemblance with the end of his story as well - ready as he was to get absorbed out of this world in few seconds.

As he stood there thinking all this, Rajeev felt a gentle touch on his shoulder. A voice said, "What's the problem with you, young man? Are you waiting for someone or do you need any help?". Rajeev turned back to look at who this person was and found an old man in a pale grey coloured shirt and black pant, a bald head and light white beard with a pleasant smile on his face.

Irritated at the interruption, Rajeev just told the old man to leave him alone.

Old man : "My child, I presume you are concerned about something in life and I can read on your face you are about to take some drastic step!!"
Rajeev snapped, " This should not bother you at all!"
Old man : "Maybe, I can be of help to you. Please come with me and I can introduce you to someone who can change things for you. I assure you, if you are not in agreement, then I shall leave you back here for you to decide what to do next."

Rajeev thought for a second and decided to give it a try, as he had all the time to execute his choice. From an end, Rajeev thought of giving it a bend. Rajeev, accompanied by the old man, travelled in the old man's car for the next one hour and reached a cottage in an isolated place. It was located in between large trees with lots of dry leaves spread on the ground, monkeys jumping over the branches of the trees and birds chirping. Both of them walked towards the cottage. The old man knocked at the wooden door, which opened with a crackling voice and there inside, was another old man with serene look, complete white hair, white moustache, white beard and dressed in a white shirt and white pant. He welcomed his friend with an intimate hug and in a low tone, inquired about the accompanying person. The old man in grey introduced Rajeev to the new person and in turn the man in white introduced himself as Tejswaroop. Tejswaroop offered both of them a warm ayurvedic herbal drink made of shrubs and dry fruits. All three sat on single seater cushion seats which were laid on the ground of the cottage at an even distance. Tejswaroop then inquired with Rajeev about the reason for his coming. Rajeev was confused, as he believed he was called in for and now he had to answer why was he here?

Observing Rajeev's perplexed expression, the old man intervened and spoke to Tejswaroop: "Sir, I found him near our favourite mountain cliff and I thought he had some horrid plans for himself; hence I brought him here."

Tejswaroop : "Rajeev, is that true? What has made you take such a decision?"

Rajeev : "Sir, with all respect to your age, it is none of your business what I do with my life. You may please not question me."

Tejswaroop : "I am no one to question you, but have you thought about what shall happen after you are gone? How will your family members reconcile with this situation? Have you protected them from at least the financial burden, if any?"

Rajeev was in complete silence. He had never thought of all this and now was seriously challenged to think over.

Tejswaroop : "I will not stop you from what you intend to do, but I can help you even in this situation by...".

Rajeev interfered : "...and how's that?"

Tejswaroop : "You do whatever you want with your life, I am concerned with the financial security of your family members and for that I have a scheme for you."

Rajeev leaned forward from his seating cushion depicting some interest in listening about the scheme.

Tejswaroop : "I am a renowned Insurance Agent. What I can do is, take an insurance policy of Rs 10 million in your name and pay the premium. You have to make me the nominee of the policy. As per the guidelines, policy amount is not payable in case anything happens to the insured in the first year. Hence you shall be taken to my COL and you can stay there for one year. You shall have complete freedom to live your life. Post this, on a pre-determined date, you shall be brought over here and then your journey shall be to the ultimate that you already have decided for yourself now. By you postponing this decision, there will be Rs 10 million generated in the system, of which 50% shall be paid to your family and the balance 50% shall be retained with me. In this manner, your life shall become helpful to your parents as well as to me. For this, in return, I shall take care of you for one year."

Rajeev was completely confused, but equally excited as his gambling mind started working vigorously. He had found an ultimate gamble with life, that would benefit his family financially.

After a detailed discussion with Tejswaroop, Rajeev agreed to this scheme of events only with an assured confirmation that half of the money shall go to his family members. Tejswaroop immediately got the entire documentation done, arranged for a medical check-up of Rajeev, made an adoption document to record Tejswaroop as his foster father and Rajeev as his adopted son. All documents were in place within 72 hours and the insurance policy of Rs 10 million was executed on the life of Rajeev. Rajeev stayed all along these days with Tejswaroop, but could never get to know the old man or his intentions properly.

After a period of seven days, a visitor approached Tejswaroop and had some discussions with him. After this, Rajeev was instructed to go to COL along with the visitor. Rajeev inquired about COL and was told that it's called the "Centre of Living" and it had few others like him over there, waiting for their pre-determined date. Rajeev started hating Tejswaroop, as he felt that he had made a business out of the ill-fate of others and what a sulphurous way it was of making money!!!

Anyhow, as he was bound by the agreement with Tejswaroop, he had to go to COL and live there for the remaining decided days. Rajeev reached the COL and found that it was a guest house built on the outskirts of a village and the ambience was like that of a hermitage, a peaceful place in the midst of greenery and birds chirping like music to the entire surrounding and prayers to the God. Rajeev was guided to a small room which had a bed, a table and a small cupboard. Three pairs of clothes were given to him and a schedule paper was handed over to him. Rajeev sat on the bed and went through the schedule paper. He was shocked to read what was written on it. It was a daily time table that he had to follow. It started with waking up at 5.00 am, followed with prayers and meditation from 5.30 am to 6.30 am, breakfast at 7.00 am, rest time till 8.30 am, working in a 'home for abandoned children' from 9.00 am to 6.00 pm with one hour lunch break during afternoon, evening prayers at 7.30 pm, dinner at 8.15 pm and getting back to the room at 9.00 pm.

Rajeev was perplexed. Why should his life be regularized when he had to live for only twelve months?

Rather, he felt that in such a situation, he should be given the freedom to live without any rules and regulations. He thought of talking to Tejswaroop about this. However, he wasn't given that liberty to speak to Tejswaroop and was instead told that he had no choice but to abide by the rules of the COL. Being an experimentalist in his life, Rajeev thought of giving this a trial to see if it would help him in doing something to keep him engaged for the coming months.

Rajeev started with his schedule from day one. Even though he found it difficult initially, over a period of 21 days, he got accommodative to the schedule and was comfortable with his early mornings. He slowly started loving working with the children. He started understanding the meanings of prayers and his faith started building confidence in him. He started growing in devotion to God and through his work of taking care of the abandoned children, he started offering sincere prayers to God. He started seeing a soul of God in every child and wanted to make a positive impact in every child's life.

Rajeev gained love and affection from all the children in the Centre. The care-taker of the Centre, Ms. Chitra had been a silent observer of this radical change in Rajeev and the way he had been making a positive change in the Home, thereby bringing vibrancy amongst the children. She started working on various child development programs closely with

Rajeev. This association got Rajeev and Chitra together and they got to know each other better. They developed a liking for each other and never knew when this liking got converted to love for each other. Rajeev, forgetting that his life itself was on a lease with Tejswaroop, started dreaming of a life with Chitra and living a life for the children of the Centre.

Time flew and the thirteen months duration of Rajeev got completed. Now it was time for Rajeev to meet Tejswaroop for the next action plan, which he had already agreed. Something which he had willingly agreed a year back, today he dreaded even thinking of it. He didn't know how to handle his situation; however he also knew that he had no choice!!!

Rajeev was communicated by COL caretaker that his meeting with Tejswaroop was fixed after three days. During these three days, his time was scheduled as

- day 1: Go to the House of abandoned children,
- day 2: Complete rest for him and introspecting his past 1 year,
- day 3 : meeting with Tejswaroop.

Rajeev couldn't sleep that night, thinking about what will he communicate to Chitra and how will he face the children?

The next morning, Rajeev got up with a perturbed mind. He had no courage to face the children and

Chitra, nor had words to speak to them. He was engulfed with emotions that lead to complete silence, but there was a volcano ready to burst inside him. He reached the Centre at 9.15 am with a disconsolate face. He first met the children. He shared some chocolates with them and hugged each one of them expressing his affection, knowing very well he may not get a chance to see them anymore. He met Chitra separately in her office. He sat silently on a chair placed across the table where she was seated, just having an eye to eye communication in complete silence. He placed his palm over her palm with tears soaking his eyes, and just kept looking at her for few minutes. Even after her inquiring the reason, he maintained his silence. Then, all of a sudden, Rajeev got up and without looking back, just walked out of the office and straight out of the Centre. Chitra was baffled with his odd behaviour.

Day 2: Rajeev got up early as usual and spent the whole day in meditation, without speaking to anyone. He just tried his best to keep the volcano inside him dormant. He spent the entire day under the supervision of the caretaker.

Day 3: As planned, Rajeev was to present himself before Tejswaroop, who would then instruct the next action plan for Rajeev who very well knew what was in store for him. Rajeev was escorted in a vehicle by two persons who had come from Tejswaroop's residence to receive Rajeev. Under complete care, Rajeev was driven to Tejswaroop's residence and was seated in an isolated room. The room had dim lights and in the center of the room was a table and two chairs placed facing each other. Rajeev was still in his silence awaiting the time for events to start unfolding as expected. After a long time, Tejswaroop entered the room. He had a small bottle and a glass in his right hand and a writing pad in the other. He placed the bottle, glass and writing pad on the table and with a smile on his face, placed himself in the chair placed opposite Rajeev.

Tejswaroop : How have been your past 13 months?

Rajeev : What's the use discussing that?

Tejswaroop : In that case, let's not waste time. Let's get straight to business. As per our deal, today is the day. Take a paper from the writing pad, write a suicide note reasoning that you do not see any meaning in living like this and thereby are voluntarily ending your life. In the meantime, I shall get this poison in the bottle poured into glass. You may consume this and end your life here itself. The rest shall be handled by me."

Saying this, Tejswaroop handed Rajeev the writing pad containing a blank paper and a pen that was affixed on the writing pad. He removed gloves that were kept in the pocket of his trousers and wore them over his palms to cover his hands. He then lifted the bottle, uncapped it and emptied the brownish thick liquid into the glass. Having done that, he stared at Rajeev without any expression.

Rajeev : "I beg to differ. Is it necessary to do this? I know I am bound by my own agreement with you and for this you have given me time and spent a lot of money on me over last 13 months. However, I would wish to express that my thoughts about life have completely changed. Earlier, when I first met you, I had no reason to live and in that anxiety, I agreed to your terms. But, the last 13 months have changed my life. Now I have reasons and purpose to live. I have a purpose of serving the abandoned children and I find my expression in doing it. It has become my thanksgiving and prayer to God. Besides, a lady has walked into my life and has filled it with love - a beautiful feeling which I had never experienced before. Hence, I have found a reason and purpose in my life. In such a situation, should I end my life? My life itself is God's gift to me and I should not end it when he has started fulfilling the meaning of it. I beg you to let me go."

Tejswaroop, in an angry demeanour, got up from his chair, leaned towards Rajeev and in a stern voice spoke: "I do not want to hear any excuses. You have confirmed to me the action 13 months in advance. This life is a life of lease given to you by me. You had no right to search for a reason and purpose in it. What I gave you, I shall decide when and how to take back. These feelings are only for the sake of time and shall fade with time. Stick to what your commitment is."

Hearing this, Rajeev begged to Tejswaroop, "My commitment is towards my life and I want to live it with the children. Please let me go."

Not hearing a word of what Rajeev said, Tejswaroop lifts the glass and firmly extends it towards Rajeev saying: "Don't force me to open your mouth and pour this in. Keep your word - drink this and end this emotional drama."

Rajeev drawing his chair backward and pulling himself behind to avoid the glass, joins his hands pleading, even as tears keep rolling down his cheeks: "I beg of you, let me live."

In a surprising turn of events, Tejswaroop stands up straight. He holds the glass in his hand and says: "If that's the case you are not leaving any option to me than…."

Leaving his sentence incomplete, he drinks the entire content of the glass himself. Rajeev is stunned to see this and jumps out of his chair to pull out the glass from Tejswaroop's hands, but by then Tejswaroop empties the entire glass.

Rajeev exclaims in astonishment: "What did you do Sir and why?!"

Tejswaroop replies with a smile, "Is there any harm in drinking a mixture of beetroot and carrot juice?

Hearing this, Rajeev gets speechless and even feels stupid at the way events start unfolding.

Tejswaroop continues: "I was just testing you to see if your interest towards life is superficial or have you really found a meaning in your life that provides you a reason and purpose. I am convinced that your thoughts are genuine and I am happy for you. Go my child, live your life, it is God's gift to you. The way you live should be your gift to him."

Tear of joy started dripping from Rajeev's eyes and a smile spread on his face. He stepped forward and hugged Tejswaroop. He kissed his right palm and slowly pushed himself down to Tejswaroop's feet. His tears were soaking Tejswaroop's feet as if he was washing the feet of the Lord.

Tejswaroop lifted Rajeev to make him stand straight, hugged him and said: "Bless you, my child. Let God take care of you, always."

Tejswaroop made Rajeev sit on the chair so that he could be pacified from the emotional outburst.

After a few minutes of gaining over his emotions, curious, Rajeev asked: "Why did you do all this to me?"

Tejswaroop explained "It's not only you, every person in COL goes through the same. We get all those persons who do not understand the meaning of life and want to end this gift of God. I and few of my friends identify such people and bring them over here. We put them through this test. What we have understood is that the biggest healer is Time and Space. When time is given, the person goes in search of answers to the questions raised by his inner voices. Space is required to unfold these answers to him meaningfully. Our task is to provide both "Time and Space", whereby the person's inner potential comes out with a purpose which brings an urge to live for others. A life which is focused towards serving others, gains over the time and space and resembles itself with the work of God."

Tejswaroop took a deep breath and continued: "We as a team of four members have come together to found this institution called COL and we look forward to changing lives and give them a meaning worth living."

Rajeev still had a question in his mind which he reluctantly asked: "How come you got into this process. Is there anything that made you start this institute?"

Listening to this, Tejswaroop's eyes got filled with tears. He removed his spectacles to wipe his tears and sat down on the chair with his face focussing downward to the floor and in complete silence. There was pin-drop silence in the room for two minutes.

Rajeev placed his arm on Tejswaroop's shoulder and squeezed it gently to comfort him. Tejswaroop regained himself; wiping his tears he sat straight and spoke: "I was a successful businessman whose only motive was to earn money. Money was the only thing that made me happy and I went in search of more happiness, ignoring the needs of family. It was unmanageably late when I realized that family requires quality time and space for every relation to build a bonding with respect. I starved them of my time and never gave them their space as my expectations on them were highly imposing. My 18 year old daughter, unable to handle this trauma committed suicide. My wife couldn't overcome this tragedy and passed away within few months. I was left all alone with loads of money with no use for it. I learned my lessons in a hard way. If only I would have given them my time and their space, things would have been different in our life, but my life was completely shattered. The only recourse and penance I could think of, was deciding to work towards all those who are dragged to such a situation in which my daughter was. At least by doing benefit to some lives, I will probably wash off my sins that I did towards my family. The only thing I have in this journey is my faith and the one source that holds my hand and leads me through… My God!!!

Rajeev was numbed with overwhelming emotions, not knowing how to respond.

Tejswaroop gaining his composure over emotions, got up and said: "My child, you are free now. Live your life to the fullest and thank God for every day that he adds into your life. Understand, life is precious."

He continued: "My vehicle is waiting outside for you to drop you at the House of abandoned children. Go and live a life of meaning, serving the children."

With immense happiness, Rajeev rushed outside the house. He saw a car parked outside the gates and hurriedly moved towards it. He opened the rear door of the car and looking at the driver pleaded to take him to his destination as early as possible. It was only when he sat inside that he realized that, Chitra was already inside the car waiting for him!

A life lived for others eventually finds its fulfilment and a connect to the eternal parent…our GOD.

~~~ ~~~ ~~~

Chapter 14

Sacrifice

Once during a heavily rainy day, a puppy fell into a ditch. It was struggling for its life. The ditch was filled with muddy water and the puppy was unable to lift itself up. The puppy was choking and hence couldn't even cry out. Ajinkya, a 20 year old boy, who was passing by the street, happened to see the puppy's struggle. His heart melted seeing the little pup's plight. A life struggling in front of him made him forget about the rain, the soil, the spoiling of his clothes. He went ahead and sat on his knees near the ditch and with a lot of effort after spoiling his clothes and getting wet in the rain, he somehow lifted the puppy out of the pit. Ajinkya then wrapped the puppy in his folded umbrella and walked towards his home in that heavy rain.

Having reached home, Ajinkya cleaned the puppy, wrapped it with warm clothes, and fed it some milk and biscuits. The puppy was saved. Ajinkya named the puppy Muddy, as he was found in a muddy pit.

Muddy grew up to become a loyal and loving pet of Ajinkya's and also became an integral part of Ajinkya's house. Muddy accompanied Ajinkya for his morning walk and wherever Ajinkya went, Muddy followed. They were inseparable. Four years passed by and Ajinkya was now 24 years old. His parents bought a new house and they all soon moved to the new place. Any guest visiting Ajinkya would be given a grand tour of the house. Muddy observed this behaviour of the family and like a true servant, took over the duty of accompanying any guest who roamed around the house. Muddy would insist that the guests follow his lead. He would take them around the house, into each room, walk them through the rooms and then bring them back to the front room. Muddy took it up as his duty to take around every visitor even after a year of shifting to this house. Anyone who came more than once also had to first follow Muddy; else he would get restless. Such was Muddy's involvement in the family and he took great pride in being a part of the family.

Soon, Ajinkya got a job that kept him busy from 8 am till 7pm. That made Muddy upset. Muddy would leave the house with Ajinkya and accompany him till the nearest railway station from where Ajinkya would board the train. From there Muddy would come back home and for the whole day, would simply lie down with closed eyes. As evening would set in, without any idea of the time, Muddy would walk to the railway station and wait for Ajinkya to return. On seeing Ajinkya, Muddy would let himself loose running around Ajinkya wagging its tail, hopping up towards him and licking his arms. Then Muddy would walk back happily with Ajinkya to his home with a sense of pride. This was a daily routine that went on and people around the town noticed and recognized this close love and affection of Muddy with Ajinkya.

Ajinkya now turned 28 years and his parents started looking for a marriage alliance for him. In the Indian culture, the parents and the boy visit the girl's house to see her and to understand the cultural compatibilities within both families. Once the boy and the girl express their liking and willingness to each other through their parents, then horoscopes are matched to confirm that their stars also match. If the stars match favourably, then dates are fixed for engagement and marriage.

Wherever Ajinkya and his family went to see the alliance for his marriage, Muddy would accompany them. This was not liked by many of the girls who Ajinkya met and all the proposals were rejected by the girl. Just to ensure the marriage alliance moves ahead, the family decided to split the group. Accordingly, the mother would remain at home with Muddy, while Ajinkya and his father would go to visit the girl's family. This plan worked and finally Ajinkya's marriage was fixed with Bharati.

Once the bride Bharati came home after the marriage, she didn't like the fact that a dog stays in the house, as she didn't like dogs at all. Going closer to Muddy scared her. Ajinkya's closeness to Muddy was not accepted by her as she felt it was too unhygienic to have a dog at home. Anyhow, she now was an integral part of this house and had to accept everyone in that house, including Muddy.

Once as Ajinkya was relaxing on a weekend and conversing with the family members and Bharati, Muddy approached Ajinkya rolling a rubber ball towards him. Ajinkya knew what Muddy was up to. He knew that Muddy wanted to show off his skill of catching the ball in air when it was thrown towards him. So, Ajinkya took the ball and threw it up in the air. Muddy swiftly dived and caught the ball in his jaws and ran back to Ajinkya and dropped the ball in front of him. Bharati enjoyed watching this, though she didn't express her gladness. This process of throwing the ball and catching continued for few minutes. In one such a throw when Muddy leaped forward to catch the ball, the ball accidentally slipped through Muddy's jaws and chocked him. He struggled for breath. Ajinkya panicked. He inserted his hand inside Muddy's mouth to pull out the ball, but failed. He tried some other ways to get the ball out, but all his efforts were futile. The ball got further stuck in Muddy's throat. Muddy started losing consciousness. Ajinkya picked up Muddy and rushed him to the nearby veterinary doctor. By then he felt, he may lose Muddy. The Doctor used tongs and slowly cut upon a small portion of the lower jaw of Muddy and pulled the ball upwards. The ball was out, but Muddy was still unconscious. The Doctor pressed Muddy's body and gave a blow of air through a pipe into his mouth. Muddy responded and shook his body. The doctor immediately gave him local anaesthesia near the lower jaw as there was surgery pending. Post the surgery on the lower jaw, Ajinkya was told by the doctor that Muddy may lose his voice for a few months. Muddy was brought home. He was well taken care of by Ajinkya.

Few months passed. Bharati got pregnant and the home was filled with happiness. A baby was to arrive and every member at home was eagerly waiting for the little bundle of joy to come home. After nine months, Bharati delivered a baby boy. The house was filled with joy. Few days later, the child and the mother were bought home from the hospital. Bharati made it sternly clear that Muddy will not enter the room where the child would be. Ajinkya tried to convey this in action and words to Muddy. No one knew what Muddy understood, but Muddy would never enter the room where Bharati or the child was. The little child however was attracted to Muddy and thus, Muddy would go until the threshold of the room and peep inside to get a glimpse of the child, Karan.

Months passed and Karan started rolling and then, crawling. He also developed curiosity towards a different creature always looking at him from a far distance. Karan started crawling towards Muddy. As Karan would come closer, Muddy would push himself backwards to ensure he didn't come in the range of the child's touch. This avoiding of Muddy's and the child's effort to reach Muddy turned out to be a game till the day Karan learned how to stand and walk. Now Karan's focus was to reach Muddy faster and Muddy would hide below the bed or any such place where the child could not reach him.

Seeing this struggle of Karan and Muddy, Ajinkya felt sorry for both and hence one day he picked up his child and took him closer to Muddy. He made Karan touch Muddy. Muddy simply sat there with his eyes closed, unmoving and the child started rubbing his hands gently over Muddy's soft body. Karan's, as well as Muddy's happiness knew no bounds. They both now became good friends and would play together. Muddy became like a second parent to the child, taking great care of him. Slowly, but over a period of time, this closeness was accepted by Bharati and she allowed her child to play with Muddy. The relationship flourished and they both became great friends of each other.

One day, Ajinkya planned for an outing to a nearby hill station and booked two rooms in a hotel for his family. The entire family i.e. Ajinkya's parents,

Bharati, Karan and of course Muddy, was to go together. Ajinkya drove down to the hill station. They all reached there in the evening and settled down in their rooms. There was a lawn outside the room and Karan, now 3 years old, in his own playful mood went towards the lawn. The rest of the family was busy unpacking their bags. Seeing the child moving towards the lawn, Muddy followed him. Nobody had a hint of what was in store for them in the next few moments. Karan saw a rope-like thing behind a flower pot in the lawn and in his naughtiness, attempted to pick it up. That rope was the tail end of a cobra-snake which was resting behind the flower pot in the cosy grass covered lawn. Since someone touched its tail, with a fear of a predator, the cobra raised its hood and hissed menacingly. Muddy saw this from a short distance and could feel that the snake would swiftly move towards the child and bite. Without a second thought, Muddy jumped and placed himself between the child and the snake. The snake, in its act to move forward and bite the child, ended up biting Muddy. Thanks to Muddy, the child got protected from the snake's venomous bite. In the next moment, Muddy turned towards the snake and lifted it by his jaws and cut the snake into two pieces to ensure that it would not bite any other family member.

By then, Ajinkya, who had heard the hissing sound of the snake, realized that something was gravely wrong. He rushed towards the lawn just in time to witness the entire act of Muddy's sacrifice towards his family. Ajinkya, followed with Bharati, hurried towards Karan and Muddy. By then Muddy was losing consciousness. His mouth had started frothing and his body started turning blue. With a painful cry, Muddy looked towards the child and Ajinkya. Ajinkya lifted Muddy on his lap and sat holding him tight, in grief. Muddy's tearful eyes had an expression of pride and happiness for having saved the life of the child who was sitting beside Ajinkya and playing with Muddy's tail, not realizing that these were the last few seconds of Muddy's life.

As Muddy was breathing his last, tears started flowing from Ajinkya's eyes. Muddy licked those tears and took his last breath happily in Ajinkya's arms, with Bharati and Karan besides him. Ajinkya was inconsolable in grief at having lost his loving companion of several years so suddenly. Muddy left them but he repaid Ajinkya for having saved his life.

Muddy's life was a life of purpose and his coming into the life of Ajinkya itself was to fulfil that purpose for which he was born for.

Everyone is in search of a purpose in life but there are certain lives whose purpose itself is to save others life. Muddy's was one such noble life.

Chapter 15

Adoption

Yatin was a -35-year old Mechanical engineer working with a reputed company as a Sales Manager. He lived with his wife Ananya and three-year old son Aditya. Yatin's father, Prakash, also stayed along with him. Having served as an Accounts Assistant for many years, Prakash had recently retired six months back. During his working years, Prakash was seen as a humble person, held good respect within the social community and was an active participant in many social and religious activities. Prakash's wife Jyoti had been a supportive and loving house wife but had succumbed to illness two years ago.

Life was going good and happy for Prakash as long as he was working. Once he retired, he transferred all his bank balances in the name of his grandchild, Aditya and also transferred the house where they stayed in the name of Yatin. Prakash wanted to spend the rest of his life with Aditya, and keep himself occupied in some religious activities within his community. Six months had passed since his retirement. His daily routine included, playing with Aditya, taking him around for a walk and visiting the nearby temple to spend some peaceful evening hours there. For Prakash, life was slowly revolving around Aditya, grooming this grandchild with values and spending the rest of the time in prayers to God. Ananya, however didn't consent to this, as she felt Prakash was interfering in her way of parenting and thereby influencing Aditya. For Ananya, the only way to deter Prakash was to continuously complain to Yatin about his father's behaviour and repeatedly harp upon the fact that Aditya is becoming a spoiled child due to the over protective behaviour of his grandfather. She insisted that for the benefit of Aditya's upbringing, he must be kept away from his grandfather. Ananya came up with a plan to ensure that she regained control over her son. She insisted that Aditya be put into a boarding school so that he shall be away from his grandfather's influence and shall become more responsible. It was a clever scheme - she knew that Yatin would never agree to this option and hence, when he refused, she cleverly and forcibly imposed upon Yatin the second option of moving Prakash to an old age home.

Helplessly, Yatin succumbed to this pressure-play from Ananya and thereby agreed to move Prakash to an old age home. Yatin inquired about an old age home that was a three- hour drive away from their house. After being convinced that the old age home was really good and would take proper care of Prakash, Yatin decided to move Prakash to this place. He communicated his intention to Prakash along with the reason behind such a decision. However, instead of telling the true reason, Yatin cited reasons of not having sufficient space in the house for three generations to grow together, Aditya needing more space as he was growing up and Ananya needing more time with Aditya, which she was unable to get due to work pressure. He also cajoled Prakash saying that the old age home was not too far away from their house and that they could be in touch on a regular basis, especially on all special occasions. Prakash was speechless. He could not say anything; tears kept trickling down his eyes. Prakash held Yatin's hands and gave them a gentle squeeze as if to acknowledge this decision. Soon, Prakash got up, hugged his son tight, and walked straight into his room to start packing his bags.

Prakash was ready with all his belongings that he needed to carry along. He put five pairs of clothes, two sets of footwear, day to day usable materials in one bag and in the other bag, he out all photographs and photo-albums that he cherished! They contained memories of his and Jyoti's married life, Yatin's growing up years and the new born Aditya's pictures. The bag also had a set of small clothes of a new born baby, the first dress worn by Yatin and such other knick-knacks that Prakash held close to his heart.

Prakash bid farewell to all his friends in the vicinity, as he was not sure when he would get to see them again. Even though he was just 61 years old, but he was mentally tired and felt like he had drained twenty years of life ahead of him, after Jyoti left him.

On the scheduled day, Yatin took Prakash to the old age home, called Heritage Nest. All the necessary documentation, formalities and payments was already completed in advance. Hence, only a sign off was sufficient to enrol Prakash as an in-member. Prakash was allocated a room on the second floor of the Heritage Nest, a room of 12 X 10 sq ft size. It had a bed, a small cupboard, a table and a chair. The toilet was outside, common for the entire floor's residents - four toilets shared among 16 rooms per floor. The canteen was at the ground floor that could accommodate 40 persons at a time for total 64 persons in the Heritage Nest. It also had two wall-mounted televisions on the side walls of the common hall, so that they could enjoy any of the common programmes. A recreation-cum-yoga room also located on the ground floor that was sufficient for 30 persons at a time. A medical room for first aid management and an ICU ambulance stationed with emergency medical equipment's was also provided. There was a hospital within a distance of 1 km and the Nest had a tie-up with the hospital for any emergency situation. All in all, the old age home was structured in such a manner that every resident would be able to spend more and more time with others and not be lonely, thereby vitalising the balance years of life with fun and togetherness.

Prakash, as a new member, was still in a withdrawal mode, as the pain of separation from his family still pinched him bad. He would spend more time within his room going through the albums and the photographs of his Jyoti and Yatin. In fact, he had hung their photos as wall-hangings all over his room.

Tony, one of the resident in the Heritage Nest, who was around 70 years of age was the next room neighbour of Prakash. Tony had a strange story to tell of himself. Tony was branded a criminal and had served three terms in jail for his illegal acts. He had sufficient money with him and he self-funded his stay in the old-age home. He had come here on his own wish, as he had nobody to call family. One of the rule of the old-age home was 'no discrimination' and this helped Tony get an admission in the old-age home. Besides, Tony has paid a good amount of donation as well. Nobody in the Heritage Nest associated with Tony due to his image. He had been a school drop-out and was always in the wrong friend circle. He had played many small pranks in his young age due to peer pressure, albeit not out of any liking. Once, as a group when these friends stole some money from a passer-by in midnight just for the sake of fun, they were caught by the patrolling police and the entire group was sentenced 6 months of imprisonment. This was Tony's official branding as a criminal. However, Tony repented this and wanted to have a normal life of status and respect. After being released from jail, Tony left the city and moved to another place, where his uncle stayed. This was with a hope to change his friend circle and also search some job that would help him stabilise in life. Tony's uncle had his own garage. His uncle took pity on him and provided him shelter and also encouraged Tony to start learning car repair work in the garage. Tony took interest in the work and soon became skilled in car repairs. Tony could easily fix any problem of a car that came in the garage for repair or in break-down condition.

In the neighbouring house to where Tony's uncle stayed, lived a family whose daughter's name was Susan. Susan developed a liking for Tony and Tony could easily make it out. Without losing time, one Sunday after the church mass, Tony proposed to Susan and she replied with a spontaneous yes. Both were in love. Tony shared this development with his uncle. His uncle took up this matter with Susan's father. Susan's father was a bit concerned, as Tony was just a garage mechanic and this would not result in a stable income that could ensure a smooth living. Tony's uncle was generous enough to immediately confirm transferring the entire garage to Tony, so that he becomes the owner of the garage and not just remain a garage mechanic. This assurance was sufficient for Susan's father to confirm Tony and Susan's marriage. Soon they became husband and wife. They were happy and together now. Tony was overwhelmed by his uncle's gestures, but refused to take the garage in his name as he knew the only property that his uncle possessed was this garage. Tony continued to work there as a mechanic.

One night at around 2 am, there was an emergency case of car break down that came as a frantic call to the garage. The garage boy was incidentally at the garage and he picked up the call. It was 3 kms away from the garage and the only way to reach there was by a two-wheeler. Understanding the emergency of the issue, the garage boy woke up Tony and requested if he could help him reach there, as the caller had stated a huge sum to be paid as reward for getting their car repaired. Tony and the garage boy rode on a two-wheeler and reached the destination. It was on a deserted road, away from the highway. The vehicle looked shabby, and no lights were put on, as if the vehicle was hidden and it was purposely taken off the road.

Tony approached the car and the frantic caller appeared from the near-by bushes to insist that his car be repaired at the earliest. The man had a face mask covering half his face. Only his eyes and forehead was visible. The scene, the person, the car: Tony understood that this was a site of some crime and he should not be a party to it. Tony refused to do anything, and as he backed out, the man flashed a torch light on Tony's face. The glare of the light was so harsh that Tony couldn't withstand it and thus shut his eyes. The masked person immediately recognised him and called his name, Tony. Tony was shocked. The masked person was one of his old friends with whom Tony had spent 6 months in jail. The masked man requested Tony to get the car repaired for friendship's sake, as revealed that he had been paid a hefty amount for kidnapping somebody and the person he had kidnapped was lying in the car, unconscious. He had to move out of this place in next few minutes, so that he could be out of this state before sunrise. For friendship's sake, Tony decides to help his friend, and gets the car repaired. The masked man hands over a decent amount of money to Tony and leaves. Few days later, a policeman comes in search of Tony. As it turns out, the police succeed in catching the kidnappers and now get into the process of picking up all the suspects who helped the kidnappers. Tony's past record surfaces and his kind act of that day is seen as an intentional party to the crime. Tony gets slapped with three years imprisonment. He pleads innocence, but to no avail. Tony gets arrested. At the same time, he also gets to know that Susan is pregnant. Tony knows he will not be able to see his new born for first two years of his/her life.

After Tony's arrest, Susan moves to her parents' place. She is mentally stressed about the turns in her life. She delivers a baby boy and breathes her last on the delivery-bed itself. The child, now parentless, is cared for by Susan's parents. Tony's uncle keeps sharing the child's photo with Tony every two months, so that he can know the progress of his child. Tony eagerly awaits the day of his release to meet up his son.

However, Susan's parents move out of the city to some other place just few days before Tony's last serving day at the prison. They do not leave any trace of their whereabouts. Tony is just left with 24 photographs of his son, now named Albert, with no trace where he is! After his release, Tony searches high & low for Albert, but in vain. Finally, Tony gives up this search. He feels extremely disturbed after having lost everything in life. This leads him back to the old ways of life which he had completely left. He gets along with his old time friends, who are now planning for a major attempt of robbery that shall provide them with sufficient wealth for the entire life. Tony becomes an integral part of this group. They succeed in their attempt of robbing and hiding the money in a safe place. However, they soon get caught and Tony lands in jail for the third time, this time for 7 years. Tony spends this 7 years and once released, he makes away with his booty, opens a restaurant and spends his life running the restaurant. After getting old, he sells his restaurant, gets a large sum of money, pays it to the old age home and settles in this place. However, Tony still keeps those 24 photos of his son, and whenever he feels lonely, he scans through those photos.

Once Tony happens to meet up with Prakash. Seeing him worried and depressed, Tony decides to chat up with him. Hence he enters Prakash's room and chats up with him. Prakash opens up to Tony with lot of emotion. He shares the photos of his Jyoti, Yatin and Aditya. When he shares Yatin's childhood photos, Tony is a bit taken back, as Yatin's photos have a lot of resemblance to his Albert's photo. Tony's further inquiry about Yatin's age, date of birth and other details reveals that Prakash and Jyoti could not have a child of their own due to health issues and hence they had adopted a three-year old child from a Christian missionary. The child's parents were not alive and the grand parents of the child had expired. Tony's doubts were getting clear - Yatin was his Albert only! Tony had found his son after 33 years. But now he was Yatin!!

However, Tony never shared this revelation with Prakash.

The next time onwards, whenever Yatin and Aditya would come to meet Prakash, Tony would somehow make it a point to meet up with Yatin. His love for his son and grandson was evident, but he never disclosed his identity. Tony bought lots of gifts for them. Yatin never understood why this old man expressed so much of love towards him and Aditya.

Prakash was also observant of Tony's changing behaviour. It was as if he had found a new life. He had become cheerful and was mingling with everyone. He greeted people and was willing to help others. Tony was a changed man.

One day, Prakash happened to step in Tony's room. Tony had gone in for a bath, hence Prakash decided to wait for him. As he looked around the table, he saw the 24 precious collection of photos, each encrypted as "my loving son, Albert". Seeing those pictures, the entire puzzle unlocked in front of Prakash. The resemblance of the photos and this sea change in Tony's behaviour made it clear for Prakash what relation Tony had with Yatin. However, Prakash also decided to maintain this as a secret, because of the fear of losing Yatin and Aditya.

After few days, Tony fell terminally ill. Prakash took great care of him during his illness. However, Tony did not survive for long. It was then that Prakash was forced to disclose Tony's relation with Yatin and insisted that Yatin should carry out the last rituals for his birth father.

That is when Yatin was aghast! Till then, he never knew that he was an adopted child and that Prakash and Jyoti had given their entire life to bring up this abandoned child. He was filled with extreme remorse thinking about what he did in return to Prakash – a man who had brought him from nowhere and created an array of opportunities for him. In turn, Yatin had only expressed ingratitude by throwing Prakash out of his life and house, for better comfort.

It was then that Yatin realised the vast difference between

a) Abandoning : only ungratefulness and cruelty towards the giver

b) Adopting: requiring courage, sacrifice and ability to give with no expectation

Some people appear in our life when we need them most. They love us and lift us up reminding us of the best, even when we are going through the worst. These people are the angels, the messengers of God.

~~ ~~ ~~

Chapter 16

The Auspicious Number

Once, while presenting the strategy plan to his company's management, Abhinav shared that the objectives and action plan were built to reach a net-revenue of US$ 101 million within the next five years. The management was very attentive and appreciative about the entire plan and the efforts put in by the business team. However, the Chairman of the global company, an expatriate had a specific question. He asked, "Why the number 101? Why not any other number?" To this, the Finance Director sitting next to the Chairman responded, "101 is an auspicious number as per Indian culture and hence probably the team must have rounded 100 to this number".

Abhinav was asked "Why is this number auspicious?" In reply, Abhinav just smiled and moved on with his presentation, because explaining the answer to this question in that forum would have been difficult in the allotted time schedule and also would have been too much of Indian-culture sharing for the team.

However, the question of why 101 is auspicious remained with Abhinav and he thought it apt to capture the thoughts associated to it. He assimilated his understanding from whatever little knowledge he could gather through his reading of various scriptures.

Abhinav then disseminated the reading and concluded that probably this might have come from a story which we all must have heard:

The 100th coin:

This is a story of a merchant. Once, in Uttarkashi, lived a rich merchant along with his family. He had two servants to take care of the house and a maid to take care of cooking. He had everything that was required for a luxurious living and was very happy with what he had. However, he was always engrossed in making more money and becoming richer. His wife was annoyed with his behaviour of being calculative and giving so much importance to wealth. Hence, she once decided to speak with him on this subject. She initiated the dialogue asking "Why are you not satisfied with what you have? Look at our maid. She has so little in her life; even her husband earns so little; but still she is so happy with what she has. Still both of them are so happy in their own scarce belongings and togetherness. Why do you keep hankering after more and more money?"

To this the merchant responded "That is because they are living in scarcity and have accepted it as a part of their life. They know that they cannot change their circumstances beyond this point. Hence they are just pretending to be happy with their life. I can prove this by giving them some wealth; let's see how they get busy in accumulating more."

Saying this, the merchant counted 99 gold coins, tied it in a small pouch and in the midnight, without anyone noticing him, he moved closer to the maid's house and left the pouch outside the main door. Next morning, when the maid's husband saw a pouch on the threshold of his door, he looked around, picked up the pouch and went inside the house. When he opened the pouch, he was thrilled to see gold coins within. With excitement, he counted them and found that there were 99 coins. He again counted them, thinking he had mistakenly counted only 99 coins, as he believed anybody who left would have ideally left 100 coins, and not 99.

This shortage of 1 coin made him desperate and he started aspiring for that additional one coin. From that day, he started working hard to earn extra money, save and buy that additional gold coin to make the tally to 100.

Such is the magic of numbers!

After a few days, the merchant asked his wife how was the maid and her husband. The wife had nothing to express, but only to respond in conformity that they are now more focused and were working hard to earn more. She confessed that she had no idea as to what had brought this sudden shift in their attitudes.

The merchant clarifies to his wife: "In the womb of our mother, we are always in connect with our spiritual self, our god. When we are born, this connect is lost for ever. Since then we are always in search of that spiritual connect and we make a mistake by searching the same in the outside world. This leads us to material things in life. As we earn these, the desire increases and then that desire turns to greed. This never ends, leading to the plus one to 101. However, the basic craving still remains and the day we have an inner awakening, the connect with spiritual self gets established, thereby the need to have more in the path of material desire also ends…

Till then, this additional 1 in the path of material achievement is a source of happiness and hence there is no harm in working hard to achieve that happiness."

The Wandering sheep:

A parable of a shepherd is expressed in the bible, where a shepherd who has 100 sheep takes them across the farm to graze. One of his sheep wanders away. Instead of being happy that 99 of his sheep are still there with him, he becomes concerned about that one sheep and goes to search that one sheep leaving behind his 99 sheep knowing well that these 99 would still be there when he returns. He becomes happy only when he finds the one that wandered away and brings it back to complete the 100.

This story in Bible is expressed to spread the message that God loves all and his love shall be for those who are with him and his heart shall also seek those who have wandered away and shall be happy only when he gets them back. In this context from this story, we can also decipher the simple magic of number from 99 to 100.

This is the power of the round number, as it gives happiness and satisfaction. We work hard to achieve that happiness and satisfaction; this search is what keeps us engaged and energised. We Indians understood this philosophy much better and our culture taught us to even better the happiness by converting it to delight and hence we add one additional to make it 101, thus adding to the happiness and moving towards delight. Hence that additional one becomes auspicious as it wishes most and more from completeness to delight. Hence in auspicious occasions we give Rs 101, Rs 501, Rs 1001 and so on. Be it whatever number, that additional '1' is to depict the message that we not only want you to be happy, but we want you to be delighted.

Imagine, if we all can implement this at our workplace, together our effort of delivering not only 100% but that additional extra '1' shall make our customers delighted with us and the culmination of that would be the organisation's delightful progress!!! **Happy 101%. God Bless!!!**

Chapter 17

Positive Humour

In India, most residential colonies celebrate Ganesh festival by arranging various cultural programs spread over five to eleven days. This story is of one such residential complex that had more than four hundred families residing within itself. Every year, this complex would celebrate Ganesh festival with lots of fun, gaiety and unity. On Ganesh Chaturthi (Birthday of Lord Ganesha) they would get a Ganesh idol made of eco-friendly material, install it with appropriate rituals, and make offerings of garlands, fruit and sweets. A separate stage would be built to conduct cultural and entertainment programs in the evening. These would include, singing completion, dance competition, theme drama, group dance, fancy dress competition and so on.

During one such celebration, the youngsters in the complex decided to stage a play of "Ramayana" for the entire audience. They planned for it a month in advance, took the cultural committee's permission to put forward this act and then identified the characters who would fit each role. The characters they had shortlisted for playing this drama were Rama, Sita, Laxmana, Hanuman, Jatayu, Ravana, Dashrath, Kaikeyi and Manthara. They decided to put up this play with just nine characters with the others supporting them in behind-the-stage and production activities.

The practice sessions continued. Absenteeism of the participants was a major concern and getting everyone together to practice regularly, was turning out to be a problematic issue. Hence, dialogues were written and given to each of them to practice on their own. The actors forgot that without team practising together, the flow could not be synchronised. But anyhow, due to shortage of time and everybody feeling that they knew Ramayan well, it was decided that one or two rounds of practicing together would be sufficient. Finally, the entire team went ahead for their act with just two rounds of practice together. The D-day arrived. Costumes were arranged and each person dressed up in the attire that their respective character demanded. The audio system was checked and the stage layout was verified just half an hour before the performance, that too with a special act where Hanuman was supposed to come on stage from a hanging rope depicting his flying ability.

The audience had occupied their place. The evening was set for the drama - The Ramayan to be presented by the teenagers. The parents of these children and other society members were waiting eagerly to watch this act. The announcement was made and the act was to start. The lights were put off and only the stage was lit with curtains closed.

Scene 1:

Kaikeyi and Dashrath were on the stage waiting for the curtain to open. The scene was the battle ground where the wounded Dashrath's chariot is driven by Kaikeyi to save the King. Pleased by this act of hers, Dashrath grants her two wishes that she can ask. The backdrop of the stage was a battle ground scene.

However, alas, even though both actors were ready, the curtain was not opening as there was a technical snag and the rope that was pulling the curtain got jammed due to getting entangled somewhere. The curtain operator was trying his best to open it, but was repeatedly failing in his attempt. In the meantime, the audience started getting impatient and began yelling and whistling. The announcer was trying to keep the audience cool by requesting them to keep silence and announcing that the play shall start in just few seconds. In the meantime, from the backstage, Hanuman, Ram, Sita, Ravan walked onto the stage to see what the confusion was all about. As the six of them were on the stage with no progress, Ram and Hanuman decided to try their hands over the weapon fight, even as Ravan and Dashrath started testing their muscle power and Kaikeyi and Sita stood at the side of the stage chatting with each other. Just then, the curtain opened and the first scene viewed by the audience was a fight between Ram and Hanuman, a wrist-fight between Ravan and Dashrath and two ladies Kaikeyi and Sita chatting. Everybody burst out laughing! The team was taken aback and rushed to take their positions. Dashrath and Kaikeyi took the centre stage and rest all disappeared from the stage. The play thus started.

Dashrath acted as an injured king who has just alighted from his chariot and Kaikeyi was the warrior charioteer who had saved the King from the battle field. Pleased by her service, Dashrath says: " Kaikeyi, I am touched by the valour you depicted on the battle field. I am even happy for the presence of mind shown by you in saving my life and I am humbled in gratitude for this act of yours. I grant you two wishes, ask what you want."

Kaikeyi : "O King, you are tired and need some rest. Thank you for your generosity and permit me to ask for my wish when I need it."

Dashrath : "So be it."

Two persons runs cross the stage holding the curtains to end scene 1 and cover the stage, as the string mechanism of the curtain had failed.

Scene 2:

The curtains are again manually opened.

The backdrop is of a palace and a room of the queen. Manthara, the maid, is with Kaikeyi. Manthara is filling Kaikeyi's ears against Ram, explaining her how Ram would ill-treat his step-mother once he becomes the King, how he may treat his step-brother Bharath as a servant of his and how Ram's mother would treat Kaikeyi like a servant. Initially Kaikeyi is shown as a casual listener and later her face expression changes as she gets carried away by what is being told to her. Her anger and dejection is expressed on her face and in her body language. The person playing the role was doing a fabulous act. Kaikeyi gets convinced that on becoming King, Ram may do harm to her and in that instance, she decides to use her two wishes. Hence she moves from the centre of the stage to a corner of the stage where she is shown expressing her grief and anger. She sends across the message through Manthara that she needs to meet King Dashrath as she needs to demand the two wishes granted to her long back.

Dashrath comes on the stage from the other corner and walks to the centre of the stage. Looking at Kaikeyi, he asks: "What is disturbing you my adorable queen? How can I help you?"

Kaikeyi demands : "Oh King, the Suryavanshis are known to keep their word. I Kaikeyi demand the two wishes that you granted me long back."

Dashrath : "Ask and your wish shall be fulfilled."

As he completed the sentence, he felt like sneezing because of the false moustache hair entering his nose even though he was avoiding and ignoring it for quite some time. He couldn't hold on anymore and sneezed so impactful-ly that his made-up moustache and beard flew off and landed on Kaikeyi's lap! Kaikeyi, who was acting her role of an agitated queen, laughed out loud and got up to help Dashrath put on the moustache and beard again. The audience had a second round of laughter from the scene. Somehow those two on the stage managed to put back the scene with Kaikeyi controlling her laughter and going back to her role and Dashrath acting out the rest of the scene with one hand holding his moustache and beard.

The scene ended with Kaikeyi asking her two wishes of making Bharat the crown prince and sending Ram on exile for 14 years. Dashrath in grief and pain agreed to these two wishes.

Scene 3:

Ram, Sita and Laxmana are getting ready to go in exile for 14 years. It was performed normally with no mess up and hence it brought the audience to a serious note.

Scene 4:

While in exile, Ravana is abducting Sita and taking away Sita to Lanka. Jatayu attacks Ravana and in turn, Ravana injures Jatayu. This scene also was performed precisely. All actors were looped into the act with utmost seriousness and the audience were tied to their seats.

Scene 5:

Ram and Laxman go in search of Sita where they meet with the injured Jatayu, breathing his last, communicates to Ram that Sita is taken by Ravan to Lanka. The only mess that happens here is that Jatayu, a vulture, keeps crowing like a crow! This confuses the audience and some of them start laughing. The remaining part of the scene gets managed well, where both the brothers go further to meet up Hanuman and hand over a ring to him to present it to Sita when Hanuman meets up Sita at Lanka, as Hanuman could fly and reach Lanka.

To ensure that Hanuman's face looked filled, he stuffs his mouth with a bun, so that it looks bulged!

Scene 6:

This is a critical scene, where some techniques were involved. There was a cut-out of tree kept at the back corner of the stage and at the other corner towards the front side of the stage, Sita was seated. The tree cut-out had a ladder kept behind; Hanuman was to climb and be on the top rung of the ladder. Seeing from the front, the audience would feel as if Hanuman is sitting on one branch of the tree. There was a belt tied to Hanuman's waist and the same was hooked on to a wire connected to a rope that was running across the stage, so that when the wire is pulled, Hanuman can fly down from the tree, reach close to Sita, get on to his knees and with folded hands, talk to her. The act was well planned as the stage was manually pulled open. The scene was all set and Hanuman was sitting on top of the tree on one corner and the other diagonal corner was Sita sitting in a garden-type set up. Sita was looking very sad and continuously chanting "Oh Ram, where are you?".

Hanuman had to give a signal to the rope puller, so that he could gently tug it for Hanuman to come down towards Sita and hand over Ram's ring to her to pass the message that Ram shall come soon to rescue her. Hence, Hanuman signalled the rope puller by calling: "Jai Shri Ram". The rope puller had actually messed up the ropes of the stage curtain rope and this rope; which was why the curtain was not functioning. However, he had to do something about it. Hence in an attempt, he pulled the rope hard to ensure that it worked. But alas, it threw Hanuman out of the branch and in a lightning speed, he came down from the tree ripping apart the branch structure and landed crashing down on Sita's feet, hitting his face down first. The impact was such that half of the bun that Hanuman was holding in his mouth spluttered out and the other half choked at his throat. He started coughing profusely to throw out the bun!

Sita, in order to control the situation, thus spoke: "Oh Hanuman, did you see my Ram?"

However, Hanuman, angry with the accident, replied: "Oh hell! First tell me who pulled the rope? I am not going to leave him."

The hilarious turn of events had the audience holding their stomachs in crazy laughter!

The curtains were immediately pulled and the stage was closed to ensure damage control.

Scene 7:

In this scene, Ram and Laxman and few of monkeys are shown to be waiting in the centre of the stage. Hanuman enters and communicates about finding Sita in Lanka and that they should immediately proceed to Lanka to save Sita. The stage is set, with every one waiting including Ram and Laxman. They are expressing their concern about not knowing where Sita is and also at Hanuman not having returned. Soon after, Hanuman enters from the back stage, a dilapidated form with his tail twisted, the shape of his mouth twisted with only half a bun there, marks of injury on forehead - not due to make-up, but as an impact of the fall that he had in the scene before.

Hanuman stands in front of Ram.

Ram : "Tell me Hanuman, what happened in Lanka"
Laxman goes close to Hanuman and in a polite smiling tone says : "Tell the dialogue, not what happened on the stage".

Everyone on stage starts giggling and Hanuman gets furious of the prank played on him.

Controlling himself, he says: "Oh Lord Ram, I met Sita in Lanka. We need to rescue her from Ravan and get her back."

The stage closes.

Scene 8:

The stage is set for the battle between Ram and Ravan. The character of Ravan was played by the team's captain who had a good body build and bold personality. Ram's dress code from the time of his exile is that of a hermit with a wig tied on his head and beads tied to his hair on the top. Ravan, dressed as a warrior, is now facing the hermit Ram. The troops of Ravan are fighting with the troops of Ram with their plastic swords across the stage and the centre stage is where Ram and Ravan are engaged in a sword-fight.

The friends of Ravan who were in the audience shouted, "Don't let Rama win". They knew their friend very well, as he was highly egoistic and would not let anything happen to let his ego go unfulfilled. Hearing what his friends shouted, Ravan became hell bent on not letting Ram win the battle. He grew so ferocious in the fight that he hit Ram's wig hard! As a result, the entire hair came off along with the beads! Ravan was enjoying his gaining control over Ram. He forgot that he had to restrict himself within his role and could not rewrite mythology. For his own ego satisfaction, he stood by the position fighting hard. Helplessly, Laxman and Hanuman had to interfere and win over Ravan to make him forcibly lie down to announce Ram as victorious.

Sita comes on stage and Ram occupies the centre stage where a sofa is placed. Next to him sits Sita. Laxman stands besides Ram and Hanuman squats on his knees near Ram with folded hands.

The show "Ramayan" gets completed with all goof-ups but still maintaining the tempo of the show.

Concluding comments:

The secretary of the residential colony was called on the stage to share few words about this maiden attempt by the teenagers of the society. This is what he had to share:

"A thought is not sufficient; planning, rehearsing and execution is equally important. This is what we can learn from this act. Our youngsters had an excellent thought, but they took the need to practice, lightly and it showed in the execution. Using techniques is critical but we need an expert hold on them, else we may fall flat on the face as was the case with Hanuman. Lastly, never get carried away due to your own ego, else we may forget the purpose of what we are doing and shall start chasing the road to fulfilling the ego only. Thereby others will have to intervene and bring you down. On the positive side, the team also never left the show midway in spite of all the mess that happened, thereby maintaining a desire of completion throughout."

"These youngsters, through Ramayan, have taught us all these valuable lessons and I am thankful to them. Like Ramayan, let the good prevail over the bad, let truth prevail and let unity and humility be the core of every human being. I thank each of the participants for such wonderful learning imparted and each of the audience for patiently sitting through and motivating these youngsters."

Such a wonderful positive learning the Secretary could see out of the situation where everything went wrong!

~~~ ~~~ ~~~

Chapter 18

Inner voice

Ishan, a school student, was very mischievous and always disinterested in studies. He was a nuisance to the teachers and also a trouble-maker for other students. He would barely manage to pass his exams every year. His parents also had to go through a let-down due to frequent reprimand by the school. They were equally concerned for his disinterest towards education.

Post schooling, all friends parted their ways and went ahead to pursue further studies. Ishan also managed to get through his school's final exams and got admission in a low profile college where he met with students similar to him. He was in a bad company of friends, which further made him completely disinterested in studies and also with his life.

Ishan spent most of his time with his friends. One such friend was Sudarshan, who was senior to Ishan by 2 years. He was feared by the college as a hooligan who would not stop at doing anything. He was known for taking up fights with everyone in the process of establishing himself as the leader within the students. Being a member of Sudarshan's group, others feared Ishan as well. Ishan mistook this as a status and enjoyed touting that power around. Hardly did Ishan realise that this would not lead him anywhere except towards bad repute.

Sudarshan's recognition as a power-leader reached the ears of the local political party, who elected him as the leader designate of their youth wing. This made Sudarshan more powerful. His close associates, including Ishan, also started enjoying the fruits of this show of power. Initially, money started flowing in through the political party for these young boys. The boys were suddenly flushed with money that they couldn't handle and hence began mis-utilising it by showing off. Soon, their lifestyle became so extravagant that they became perennially in need of extra money. This was the time where the political party started demanding deliverables from these boys. Just for the sake of money, they yielded to those demands.

The demands were to get the political party established in the college to promote and propagate their existence, as well as, convert the vote bank of students, teachers and their families in favour of the party. This was not a major demand - Sudarshan and his friends could easily take care of it.

The next demand on these boys was to become a united force to provide security to real estate builders against other such parties. The deal for money to provide such a security mechanism was already agreed by the political party and the real estate builder. The boys had no idea how much booty was involved in this transaction. They were risking their life under the banner of political warfare amongst two groups.

Unaware of what was in stake for them, the boys continued doing this as they were getting paid handsomely for their 'services'. As college students, enjoying a political backing, money in the pockets and ability to deal with big business houses in the realm of real estate, soon put their heads in the clouds. They soon got carried away with money, power, fame and position.

By then, five years had passed and now the final year exams of the college were round the corner. Everyone were busy preparing for their exam, except for Sudarshan and his friends, as they believed that they didn't need exams and certificates to establish themselves. They felt that politics was their career and they could easily make it big in life by continuing in this line.

Ishan too got carried along with this thought of Sudarshan and was a key person in Sudarshan's activities. After all, since the last four years, the boys had earned a spoilt living through their hooliganism.

Then one day, there came up a deal where the portion of land was under dispute. The political party summoned Sudarshan to get the land vacated as they had already struck a deal with one of the real estate builder to get it vacated for commencing construction at the site. Sudarshan and his two trusted friends including Ishan went to the site for inspection. They noticed that the land was fenced and used as a parking ground by some local influential group who had a claim on that land. In order to establish superiority over the group and establish forceful control over the land, Sudarshan and his friends started pulling down the fence. In rage, they smashed the glasses of one car parked on the disputed land. Through their actions, they had demonstrated a clear message that they shall not spare anyone messing with them. People started crowding at the area to see what was happening, but no one dared to stop these guys. Sudarshan warned everyone, "Dare not step onto this piece of land. We shall get a bull-dozer and get this entire land cleaned. If these vehicles belong to any of you, better take them out, else we may not care for any vehicle inside when we take charge tomorrow."

The next evening, Sudarshan and his team landed at the site in two SUVs. This time they thought they were well equipped, as they had a larger team of ten members, hockey sticks, knifes and a bull-dozer to raze the disputed land and put the board of the person whose work they were executing on behalf of the party. When they arrived at the site, the site looked as it was left by them the previous day. The cars were still there, the glass-shattered car also was there, the fence that they had pulled down was also in the same form as they left. This angered Sudarshan further. He jumped out of the car, pulled out a hockey stick and ran towards the site. His friends also got into action. Never did they realise that today the parked cars were not empty. There were already people seated inside. Sudarshan and his friends were caught unaware. Sudarshan headed towards the first parked car. He raised his hockey stick and broke the back glass. To his utter surprise, in a split moment, the back door of the car opened and a man leapt out of the car firing a bullet at Sudarshan. The notorious group on the other end was more prepared than Sudarshan and his gang. The latter were caught completely unaware that they had been lead into a trap! Sudarshan was hurt in his knee. Seeing their leader hurt, a war of rage ensued between both the groups. However, their hockey sticks and knives couldn't stand for long in front of the country-made revolvers that the other group was carrying along with bamboo sticks and iron rods. The street fight continued for the next 15 minutes till one more round of firing could be heard. Nobody knew who got hurt in the process, till Sudarshan fell down bleeding and struggling for his life. This scared his group and they began fleeing from the site in panic. They rushed to the SUVs and drove back hastily for their lives. The attack was a major jolt for Sudarshan's group. The crime was reported, police got involved and necessary actions were taken to file a complaint. Ishan and his friends got a sentence of two years in prison for their criminal act.

Once out of jail, the group met again. This time they had a major vacuum as they had lost their leader and nobody else in the group had the guts or the courage to stand up and fill that void.

Ishan was left in despair. He had wasted precious eleven years of his life, taking it easy and not doing anything productive. What he believed as his path of life had suddenly come to an end with the death of Sudarshan. He had neither qualifications nor any source of revenue to survive. As luck would strike badly for him, that year he lost his father as well. Ishan now was completely broken.

He refused to move out of his house and kept wondering about what had happened to his life and how he had ruined it completely. However, finally, hunger got the better of him. Soon, Ishan started selling things from his house to get money to feed his mother and himself. His mother steadfastly refused to let him sell the house and that was the only property left now.

Soon all other material things that Ishan could sell, began getting exhausted. He had to fend for himself and his elderly mother. Having no other option and hunger striking badly, he took to begging outside a temple. The money that he got from begging, somehow barely sufficed for getting them both some food daily.

Ishan continued doing this for few months. However, his ears also continuously heard the devotional prayers, the discourses within the temple and that gave him some relief from all the dejection that he was going through. More than begging, he looked forward to hearing about God, soul, inner voice while sitting outside the temple. Slowly his mind was finding an inner peace and there was a sudden flow of serene energy that he started feeling within.

Nearly two years had passed. Ishan continued begging just for the sake of earning that food to keep his mother and him alive. His motive now, however, was completely different. His craving was to get mental calmness, to kindle a spiritual connect, to awaken his inner self. This, he could satisfy by being in touch with what he heard in silence, sitting outside the temple. His tongue chanted the mantra of God, his mind was filled with the aura of the immortal omnipresence. Ishan was not bothered what he was getting by end of the day. Whatever he got, he collected happily with gratitude and went home to wait for the next day.

Ishan started meditation and practising silence to hear that inner voice which is always suppressed due to so much of noise made by our mind. Ishan's search for himself deep inside within through continuous state of silence lead him to discover the peaceful and purposeful inner self. Through prayers, through meditation, through the way he led his life, by the purity of his thoughts and feelings, through devotion, surrender and faith, Ishan could feel thy presence of his God within his inner voice. In such a silence, once Ishan was struck with a thought: "What was the purpose of my life?"

His inner voice thus spoke to him : "Your basic necessities of life are food, clothing and shelter. Clothing is taken care by all that you already have, you already have a house of your own to provide you shelter. For food, you raise your arms and beg for your food. Isn't this is a selfish life? Everyone have their own source of fulfilling the basic necessities. The purpose of your life is fulfilled only if your life is useful to others. You have to live a life where out of you many other lives can live. Be that source of living for others, so that God shall feel proud of having created you and sent you as a human being."

Ishan's mind asked : " How can I do that? I myself live in peace out of the earning that I get by begging. How can I be a source of living for others?"

Inner voice : " First uplift yourself. Like you, there are many who have confined themselves to earning by begging. There are many who are dying hungry on the streets. Work for them."

Ishan's mind : "What can I do?"

Inner voice : "Find the answer yourself"

Ishan opened his eyes, completely shaken from his meditation. It was as if a spiritual guide had spoken to him, urging him to evolve. He felt as if he was the chosen one and he had a path to walk. For the next few days, his mind struggled to find an answer.

Ishan got his answer out of his inner voice itself. He stopped begging for himself - instead he started pleading people to give him money to feed others. He converted his house to a place where he fed those who starved and were not able to even beg for their living. It was a centre created by Ishan for giving dignity to lives of those ignored people on the streets. His centre became known for its services. People came ahead and provided him with money, grains and pulses to meet the requirement. Some also donated clothes. Ishan suddenly became a source of support for many. The space from where he operated, started falling short.

To Ishan's surprise, a corporate approached him and offered him a larger space from where he could continue his services. Now Ishan continued in the same path of taking from those who have and giving to those who don't. In a short span of three years he was well known for his services and there were multiple corporates and other social organisations who supported him in what he was doing.

His inner voice still was not satisfied, as Ishan still felt there was something missing. To find his answer, he realised, he had not spoken to the inner voice for long and hence he needed to concentrate to connect to his inner self. In silence, he tried connecting to his inner voice.

Inner voice : "You have walked far too much on this path. Aren't you missing creating a meaning in their lives?"

Ishan : "I do not get you. How can I create a meaning in their lives?"

Inner voice : "Find the answer yourself"

Ishan was again shaken by this; however, this time he pleasantly accepted this challenge, knowing very well this would lead him to some surprising pleasant outcome.

Ishan was in his thought process and the spiritual guide led him to the doors of a corporate who was willing to outsource jobs to his organisation, whereby he could arrange a source of revenue for those who were dependent on him. Now Ishan had moved one more rung of the ladder by providing dignity of living through self-earning and thereby making them self-sustainable, to all those unfortunate individuals. In turn, they collectively uplifted Ishan's organisation to ensure more and more people are provided with that hand-holding required to come out of the wretched life on the streets.

Ishan in search of food to overcome his hunger accidentally found inner peace that lead him to connect with his inner voice that showed him the path of purpose through which he became a source of living for many. In this path he realised the true meaning of God and spiritual connect, and thereby with gratitude continued to serve the people always, being humble.

We never know which turn will bring a twist in our life. So keep on walking with trust in God, as in this journey called life he constantly gives us opportunity to live with peace, happiness and a purpose.

~~~ ~~~ ~~~

Chapter 19

Love is That What Creates

35-year old Sandeep Menon was a Senior Financial Consultant with a reputed firm in Mumbai. He was blessed to have a wholesome life filled with professional success, along with personal happiness that stemmed from having a beautiful loving wife and a three-year old daughter.

Once, Sandeep had to travel to Bangalore to meet up with a client for a project discussion. He landed at the Bangalore airport and before meeting with the client, had to discuss few financial aspects with his local office representative. Sandeep was asked to meet up near the MG Road Corner coffee shop situated in a shopping mall, where both of them were to spend an hour exchanging notes before they met the prospective client. Sandeep took a prepaid taxi from the airport, got dropped at the mall, picked up his handbag and started dialling his local office representative's number via his cell-phone.

As he was talking over phone and walking by the outer passage lane of the shopping mall, he observed a small girl, around five-years old, walking out of the shopping mall as a car was reversing. Noticing with horror that the car would hit the girl, in a split second, Sandeep leapt to protect the child. He managed to push her away but at the same time, he got hit on the rear end of the car, causing the driver to halt the reversing. Sandeep's flash action saved the child but in the process, his handbag and mobile got thrown aside. Sandeep got up, collected his belongings, and rushed to see if the child was okay. The child's mother and her friend, who were walking few steps behind chatting with each other, also rushed to the scene as they had witnessed the horrifying scene from a close distance. The mother was concerned for her daughter and hence rushed to console the child. She made her feel relaxed and also assured that she was not hurt. The mother was cajoling her weeping daughter as the child had started crying in shock of what happened in the last few seconds. By then, Sandeep also got closer to the child and soothed her saying, "I hope you are safe now. There's nothing to worry, my child."

The mother wanted to thank Sandeep. She looked at him to utter the words 'Thank You' and suddenly, she just couldn't say anything! She kept looking at him shell-shocked! . By then, Sandeep also looked at the woman and was taken aback. 'Oh, it is Sandhya!' he mused, recognising her instantly. Eleven years of separation had not managed to erase the loving and deep-rooted memories that they both held within their hearts. Mere seconds of staring at each other brought back an instant flash of five years of togetherness and eleven years of separation. Both of them relived all the emotions in those few seconds.

However, soon after, they both got aware of people staring at them and thus, maintaining silence, went their separate ways. Sandeep wished he could turn back and catch a few more glimpses of his Sandhya, but he restrained himself to avoid any emotional outburst.

Sandeep reached the coffee shop where his office representative was waiting for him. They had a meeting, then went to meet the client, had a detailed discussion and then Sandeep returned to the airport that evening. He never realised how the day went, what happened and how did the discussion progress, as his physical presence had nothing to do with his mental and emotional presence that were already running amok through the memory lanes.

At the other end, after the incident, when Sandeep walked away, Sandhya was still in a state of shock for few more seconds. She tried losing herself in the crowd of the shopping mall, holding her daughter tightly in her arms with tears rolling down, not sure about the real reason behind the tears!! Sandhya's friend Roshni, observed a few visiting cards of Sandeep lying on the floor where he leapt to save Sandhya's daughter Amrita. Roshni picked up the cards and kept them in her purse. Roshni consoled Sandhya and drove them both back home. Roshni still felt that the incident that happened at the shopping mall was instrumental for Sandhya's state.

After reaching Sandhya's home, Roshni made them both sit comfortably and got some water to drink. After confirming that Amrita was relaxed, Roshni told her to go and play. Roshni noticed that in spite Amrita being back to normalcy, Sandhya was still in a withdrawn state. Roshni hugged her friend tight, causing Sandhya, who was holding back her emotions, to burst out in tears. She cried like a baby in Roshni's arms. Roshni was perplexed, not knowing what this was all about.

Roshni shook Sandhya and said: "Sandhya, calm down. Why are you so upset about it? Nothing major has happened to Amrita. That man saved your daughter's life and Amrita is perfectly all right. Why are you still in pain?"

In weeping tones, Sandhya finally spluttered: "That man......that man...you don't know, he...he is the cause of my pain. He has saved Amrita but, but left me in despair..."

Roshni : "What are you saying? What did he do? He put his life in danger to save your daughter, didn't even utter a word and walked away as if nothing happened. Where did he?...."

There was a pause in the conversation and then Roshni continued: "Wait a minute, do you know him? Yes, there was a dead silence between both of you, but your eyes were communicating a lot. I get it! Tell me if I can help you?"

Sandhya replied : "No, you don't know anything. It's my deep ingrained pain that I have to live with through-out."

Roshni in perplexed situation : "Whatever it is, if you don't want to share with me, it's your choice. But let me know in case you need any help from me. By the way, there were few cards that flew from that gentleman's pocket. I have picked them up. I am leaving them here for you; probably they may open a gateway to peace." Saying this Roshni kept the visiting cards on the table, picked up her bag and left.

After Roshni left, Sandhya immediately picked up the cards and kept them in her bag. She went into her bedroom and sat there with tears in her eyes and a slight smile on her face., as she started travelling down the memory-lane.

Sandhya's mind went 16 years back. She was 17 years old then. She remembered the day very clearly when she had gone to meet one of her school friend, Manish, on his birthday. Other than few school friends, Manish had also invited few of his personal friends. One such friend was a very timid guy, standing in a corner, not talking to anyone, only flapping through a book that he was holding. Sandhya, a bubbly person, was introducing herself to everyone. She was very beautiful for her age and the dress she wore was making her much more attractive. All boys in the party had an eye on Sandhya and Sandhya liked the attention that she had garnered in the party. Manish was eagerly waiting for few more guests to join. Manish went to that timid, shy boy and asked him to set up the cake on the table. It was only then that Sandhya noticed this boy, as she missed him completely while being introduced to all. She boldly approached him and said: "Hi, I am Sandhya." She extended her hand for a hand-shake. He politely folded his arms in Namaste and said " Hello, I am Sandeep. Excuse me, I have to arrange the cake for Manish." Saying this, he left.

Sandhya was taken aback, as she felt Sandeep was rude and he never knew how to talk to a lady. Anyhow, the party continued and there were couple of occasions where Sandhya and Sandeep came face to face and both ignored each other.

A few days went by. Sandhya and two of her other friends happened to meet Manish at his residence. They were chatting and having a good time. Manish shared the photos of his birthday party. In one of the photo, Sandhya noticed Sandeep's photo and in a slight angry tone asked Manish: "Isn't this Sandeep? The arrogant guy, who doesn't know how to behave with people?"

Manish looked at Sandhya and started laughing. She said: "I am serious, why are you laughing!?"

Manish : "I am enjoying seeing the emotions of two people towards each other!!"

Sandhya had a question mark on her face.

Manish then went to his cupboard, took out a framed packet, handed it over to Sandhya and asked her to open it right then. She opened it and found a photo-frame with a beautiful sketch of hers inside it. The sketch was impressive and it brought a beautiful smile on her face. Astonished by the art, she asked Manish: "Who did this?"

Manish : "The person's name is signed below."

Sandhya observed that it was signed as Sandeep and she didn't believe it! She just kept the photo-frame aside and said: "This is rubbish."

Manish : "What? The sketch, the person in the sketch, or the person who did the sketch?"

This made Sandhya think. She asked : "Why would that silly Sandeep do it? He didn't even have the courtesy to speak to me properly that day."

Manish : "That's where you are mistaken, Sandhya. Don't judge him before knowing him. Sandeep is a close friend of mine for the past five years. He is elder to me by two years. We play football together for the same team. That's how I came to know about him. Five years ago, Sandeep came in the football junior team of our club. He was introduced to the team by our coach. Our coach, while watching a match played between two orphanages, identified Sandeep's potential and introduced him to the team. The coach took nearly one year to arrange for sponsorship for Sandeep. The coach not only got Sandeep's football sponsorship, but also arranged for his education. This is Sandeep. He is very timid, he is very shy of facing people, he likes to be lonely, he seldom speaks, and he hardly has any friends. Every day he plays his role in the football team quietly and never stays back after practice, as he has no money for refreshments. His best friends are me and the goalkeeper of our team and a few friends of his college where he is studying for Commerce graduation. He has other few hobbies as well, like he is good at sketching, he works part time at the Library nearby from 2.30 pm to 5 pm to earn some money. After football practice, he goes in the late evening to teach swimming, to earn some more. All this he does so that he need not burden his sponsors for money and can also save money for higher studies. I hardly remember him speaking about any girl. That day after the party, I caught him sitting alone and smiling and this expression, I never had seen on my friend. On inquiring, he never shared anything and just walked away. Five days later he came to meet me with this packet and said, "give it to your friend Sandhya as a thanksgiving for making me realise that I also have a heart within me". That is how this packet has come for you."

Sandhya was spellbound. Suddenly her impression about Sandeep changed from earth to the sky in jet-speed. She took back the sketch, looked at each stroke of the pencil and started admiring the way it captured her expressions.

Sandhya wanted to know more about Sandeep; hence she joined the library where he was working part-time. Sandeep felt it was a coincidence, but it was too true to be a coincidence when he saw her again at the swimming pool late in the evening having registered her name to learn swimming. The library and swimming lessons gave both of them proximity to meet continuously two times a day and these meetings soon turned into love. Sandhya was waiting that Sandeep would propose, but months passed, a year passed, but Sandeep didn't propose at all. Sandhya felt either he was not understanding her feelings, or she was wasting her time.

One of those days, Manish happened to visit Sandhya to chat with her. Knowing from Sandhya that they both had been meeting regularly, but Sandeep had not proposed to her yet, Manish handed over an envelope to Sandhya and said: "I don't know what's in this, but probably you may find your answer."

Sandhya opened the envelope hastily. Inside was a small note from Sandeep that read: "My love for you is immense, but I also know that between fantasy and reality, cruelty prevails and I don't want to pain you in any manner. For your own benefit and future goodness, it is better that we don't get into any relation. Wish we wouldn't have met. You are serene and beautiful. I would love to see you like that for life time. But I may not be able to fulfil your dreams. Your admirer…"

Sandhya just looked up towards the roof wondering what to do. She looked at the wall clock hanging in her drawing room. It was 2 pm. She knew she could get Sandeep at the Library at 2.30 pm. Sandhya asked Manish to accompany her to the Library. They reached at around 2.45 pm. Sandeep was arranging the books on the shelf. Sandhya and Manish walked inside the library. With rage in her voice, she asked Sandeep to look at her. Her thundering voice in the silent library made everyone turn towards those three. As Sandeep turned towards her, she swiftly hugged him and announced "I love you, you stupid!!"

Everyone in the library clapped and some burst out laughing. Sandeep had no words! With a bashful face he looked at Manish and tried to push Sandhya away, but her embrace was so tight that Sandeep was helpless.

Their love story thus started. It was a beginning with no expectation and mutual acceptance. Sandeep loved Sandhya for her tenderness and beauty and Sandhya loved Sandeep for his sincerity, truthfulness and loyalty. Their love story was a beautiful journey. There was no Library and no swimming classes any more. The beautiful love within them flourished and blossomed for three years. It was a journey worth envying for all lovers; filled as it was with lots of care, concern, respect, appreciation, understanding, feelings and emotional expressions.

In due course of time, Sandeep completed his graduation and started pursuing a management course. Time became demanding on him. Sandeep had to become something in life before he could marry Sandhya. By then, Sandhya also got busy with her music classes. Both had their own set of new associations, they had transitioned into the next branch of their life where new horizons started unfolding before them. They could hardly meet, probably once in three months and that too would be just for a short time. During that time, Sandhya was more demanding due to her expectations from Sandeep and not being able to accept his fast-paced life. Her demands were basically towards togetherness, phone calls, outing, regular contacts, which Sandeep felt difficult to cope up with. He felt Sandhya had turned into a suffocating nag. His love for her was immense, he missed her every moment but he wasn't being able to handle her heightened expectations. Soon, the two started drifting apart.

The door bell rings. Sandhya snaps out of her thoughts. She gets up, wipes her tears and goes to open the door. She sees Satish, her husband, standing at the door having come back from his office. He enters the house with a broad smile and asks Sandhya about her day. Thankfully, he does not read Sandhya's face beholding a plethora of emotions. Sandhya quickly moves to the kitchen, makes tea and serves it along with some snacks to Satish, who is busy scanning the sports page of the newspaper.

Soon, Amrita comes running to Satish, clambers on to his lap and narrates what happened in the morning. Satish is shocked! He calls Sandhya and asks about it. She confirms. In a thanks giving and gratitude to the God he looks up to say a prayer and hugs both of them together. He empathises with Sandhya for her sad state of affairs that day and agrees to take them out for dinner that night just to make the family feel relaxed.

Meanwhile, in the flight from Bangalore to Mumbai, Sandeep also relives the precious times and the ups & downs of his life. He remembers the time when it was nearly six months to the time he last met Sandhya. His pre-occupancy with work coupled with the final stages of course completion, were taking up all his time, as he was working while doing his management course. He remembered Sandhya every day of his life. He thanked God and Sandhya for his life. He was counting the time required to complete his management studies and thereby get a respected position. He was back-living the time from the date that he had already written for himself, when he could meet up with Sandhya's parents to seek her hand in marriage.

One late evening, Manish visits Sandeep's rented house. Sandeep is thrilled to see his friend. He inquires to Manish about his purpose for coming there. Manish communicates that he has got a bad news for Sandeep.

Manish confirms that he met up with Sandhya just few days back and she wanted him to communicate this message to Sandeep. Her message was that 'she is not interested in someone who disrespects her and has no care or concern for her. If Sandeep is not interested in her, even she does not care for him. She has already decided to walk away from this relation and it is better if he also stays away from her'. Manish continued saying that she wants all her letters and photos back and that Sandeep dare not try to contact her anymore.

Albeit shocked, in a composed manner, Sandeep collects all her photos, and letters, hands them over to Manish and requests him to leave. Making sure that Sandeep would be okay, Manish reluctantly leaves from his room. The moment Manish leaves, Sandeep closes the doors and weeps like a dam that opens up the flood gate! He feels that his life has come to an end. He has no more reason to live for anyone. He just stops studying and goes out of the house at midnight, not knowing where he is heading towards. He walks for some distance but still unable to overcome the distress, he starts running on the street aimlessly, just to exhaust himself. Tired and completely fatigued, he sits down somewhere at the roadside and drops off to sleeps.

In the morning, Sandeep wakes up to the sound of a sweeper sweeping the street, the birds chirping on the trees, the sunrays penetrating through the trees to touch the ground, the newspaper boys out on their cycle to distribute papers, the milk delivery boys carrying bags full of milk bottles for distribution…. The sight brings back a pleasant thought in him. 'Life doesn't stop anywhere, for anyone. There is a new beginning every day. The day ends so that yesterday can be left behind and a fresh new day can be started for a new living'. He gets up, cleans his face with the water flowing from a nearby street tap, and returns to his house with a slow jog, reminding him every moment he will do big in life, nothing will stop him.

Eleven years had passed from that day till date. Sandeep had graduated in his management studies, and had become a successful Senior Financial Consultant with a reputed firm. He got married five years back and was blessed with a beautiful loving wife, Aadhya and a three-year old daughter.

Sandeep was wondering, as to why had Sandhya come back into his life after so long?

He also started analysing as to what had gone so wrong 11 years back that they had withdrawn totally from each other. He drew a few facts as under:

a) The liking was immense at the beginning due to mutual appreciation, but it was misconstrued as love

b) Every relation starts building up expectations which are difficult to fulfil

c) Relations suffer if there is no acceptance of circumstances or person, on an 'as is where is' basis

d) Never neglect a person in the name of love

e) Love requires expression and it should be truthfully expressed

f) Love is that what creates and not what destroys

While he was lost on thought, Sandeep's flight landed at Mumbai. He took a cab from the airport, reached home and embraced his wife Aadhya and daughter. They were pleasantly surprised, but were not aware that it was Sandeep's lesson number "e" that he just learned in the flight, put to action.

Next morning, in Bangalore, Sandhya was still lost in her thoughts. Satish had left for office, Amrita had gone down to play and Sandhya was alone at home. Loneliness drove her crazy with a bombardment of emotions that she had suppressed the previous evening. She reached out to her bag and searched for Sandeep's card. . Having fished out the card, she kept staring at the cell number displayed on it, thinking whether to ring on it or not.

Hundreds of thoughts kept crossing Sandhya's mind. She was not sure of what she was up to. Not sure whether her action of calling Sandeep would lead to problems in her married life later. She didn't even know where Sandeep was at that point of life. Whether he was married or not? At one point, she even thought of calling up Manish and asking about Sandeep instead of calling up the latter directly. All sorts of questions kept skittering in Sandhya's mind. Finally at around 4 pm, exhausted by all this mental jugglery, Sandhya makes up her mind to call Sandeep directly.

She dials the number and holds on. The phone gets connected.

Sandhya : "Can I speak to Sandeep?'
Sandeep : "Yes, Sandeep speaking. May I know who is this?"
Sandhya : "Eleven years is a long period to remember the voice, isn't it?"
Sandeep : "Eleven years two months and five days, to be precise."

A short silence prevailed communicating many unsaid emotions.

Sandeep : "How's your daughter now? What's her name?"
Sandhya : "Are you married?"
Sandeep : "Question in response to a question?"
Sandhya : "Her name is Deepa. We call her Amrita at home, that her pet-name. She is fine now. She is thankful to the Uncle who saved her life and so is her mother, for everything in her life."

Sandeep : "Deepa, good name. You have just tweaked my name and removed 'S' and 'N' from it. Do you still care for me!!"

Sandhya held back her emotions hidden in her voice and responded back with her question: "You have still not answered my question. Are you married?"

Sandeep : "Yes. I have a loving wife and a three year old adorable daughter named Shama."

Sandhya felt relieved from the guilt that she was carrying till date regarding Sandeep's well-being. She then responded: "Where have you forgotten me? Your daughter's name shares a similar meaning with my name."

The same silence prevailed for two seconds and Sandeep laughed, realising that he too had been caught.

The next question from Sandhya came as a thought changer for both of them.

Sandhya : "When are you next in Bangalore? Can we meet?"

Even before Sandhya finished her question, Sandeep's spontaneity affirmed to this in a sulking and deep voice.

Now Sandeep and Sandhya both looked forward to this meeting after eleven years of separation. They were oblivious of the world existing beyond them. Euphoria was in the air for these two love birds and they suddenly felt younger by eleven years.

Sandeep had to visit Bangalore for the incomplete official project; rather, he conspired the situation to land himself to Bangalore. He eagerly called up Sandhya to confirm his visit and also fixed up a time to meet her while in Bangalore. After having completed his official work, Sandeep was waiting eagerly for the moment when he would meet Sandhya. The place was the same shopping mall, but in a restaurant which hardly anyone visited from 5 pm to 7 pm.

Sandeep got ready before time. He wanted to reach the place half an hour early, so that he could relax and calm down his heartbeats before 'his' Sandhya reached. He dressed himself in the best suit that he carried with him, wearing a blazer over it to create a good impression. Today he could afford all the luxuries which he had dreamt of fourteen years back. He wanted to look the best and create an excellent impression. He was getting ready as if it was his first date. He had completely forgotten about his family, focussing only on meeting Sandhya and talking to her to relive those golden moments he had shared with her long back, the aura of love that encompassed only the two of them .....

He reached the restaurant and chose the corner table where he could talk to Sandhya peacefully. Soon, he saw Sandhya walking in. Oh God, even she had planned to reach early! Both smiled at each other. Sandeep got up and pulled the chair for her to sit. After she is seated, Sandeep takes the seat next to her, gazes at her fondly and says: "same beautiful eyes, after so long."

Sandhya looks away shyly. Sandeep looks at her from top to bottom. She also is dressed for the occasion to create an impression.

Sandeep : "How have you been all these years? Did you ever miss me?"

Sandhya : "Didn't you? You had the choice of talking to my parents for marrying me. You could have done it."

Sandeep : "It's all over now. I hope you are happy in your life. I was always concerned for your wellness and I am happy to see that you are happy and well settled in life."

Sandhya : "I am blessed, my daughter is a cute girl and my life goes busy taking care of her."

Sandeep : "My daughter is so naughty, she is the centre of everything at my house. My wife is always busy taking care of her. My wife is a beautiful person by looks and at heart. She never hurts anyone and understands and respects human relations."

Sandhya replied in an accusing tone : "What do you mean by that? That I don't respect people? Listen, it is you who disrespected me. I loved you when you really needed it so that you could build your own self-respect and create an aim, an ambition in your life. I am the reason for what you are today."

Sandeep : "I am sorry, I never meant to hurt you. I was just expressing my emotions and thoughts. I did not say it to let you down. Let's not discuss this. You have not mentioned about your life. How about your husband, what does he do?"

Sandhya : "I am happy in my life and he takes care of me well."

After a pause, Sandhya continued : "Is your wife aware about your past and our relationship? Have you mentioned about me to her?"

Sandeep : "Yes I have. My wife knows about my past and she has accepted me the way I am. Have you mentioned about me to your husband?"

The golden silence continued for some time and then Sandhya spoke : "Will you let your wife know that we met today? Will you introduce me to your wife and if so, as what?"

Sandeep was in silence after hearing this. He thought for some time. He had had a beautiful past, a serene present and a bright future and he had to choose between an option of linking his past and risking his future to an option of staying in his serene present and build the bright future. While physically he was present there with Sandhya, mentally he was disconnected.

Sandeep and Sandhya spent half an hour more in the restaurant and the discussion evolved over comparison, sometime trying to make each other feel guilty of their mistakes, sometime making each other feel how happy are they in their own lives. It was more of a formal talk that they had. They wound up the meeting and headed towards their own places. Both shook hands and walked apart in their own directions without turning back, thereby re-emphasising the closure of their relationship on a sweet note, storing the memories as a treasure within their hearts to be revisited time and again, but never to be expressed.

What they probably realised was that the past was over and it did not make any sense living in the past. The happy and sweet memories within their hearts were sufficient to last for a lifetime. Also, a major realisation they had was that each of them had a family to live with and their commitments were towards their present to build a future that is more progressive. Attaching themselves to the past which cannot be changed held no meaning in life anymore.

Sandeep proceeded towards the airport, checked in and waited at the lounge. Even amidst the crowd,

Sandeep was feeling lonely from inside. Trying to make the best out of the waiting time, he started to put things in place to understand the entire episode. He realised that it was not about Sandhya or him; it was about the divine invisible presence that conspires things for us. A Sandhya had to walk into his life to break all the inhibitions he carried within and to expose him to a world of love, respect, attraction, so that he could feel wanted. That gave him the courage to face the world boldly; it helped him in creating an ambition within himself; and to pursue it to make him what he was today. Sandhya leaving him also had a meaning that in life we should never take anyone for granted, we have to work hard to maintain relation, position, status and emotional connect. The other realisation was his family is what was destined for him and they too are so loving and caring that they make his life complete. The best is to keep distance from relationships of the past with a realisation that somewhere in the world there is a heart that cares for him. Sandhya's silence was a depiction of her love that created him and both moved on in life on their own destined path.

Some people's purpose in life is to help us grow and some come in the journey of our life to serve this purpose and move on. Sandhya was one who came in Sandeep's life, served the purpose and left. His current family is his current purpose in life and he should remain dedicated to them. This understanding relieved him from all thoughts that were crossing his mind and with a sense of gratitude to God, Sandeep sat at the waiting lounge peacefully for the announcement of flight departure.

The new journey began for him from thereon!

~~~ ~~~ ~~~

Chapter 20

Celebrating Death

Sebastian was employed with a pharma company at a leadership position with 18 persons reporting to him. He was instrumental in the brand-building activities of OTC (Over The Counter) products and hence his focus was to make his company's products appealing to the consumers/ patients. He ran a busy schedule and the only human association he had, would be with his office colleagues and customers. He came home only for dinner, sleep and some breakfast – living a hectic life typical for any pharma employee. For Sebastian, the definition of work-life balance was, 'work, so that life goes on'.

On one such busy day, Sebastian received a surprise call from his long time college friend, Kiran, whom he had last spoken to maybe two years back. Kiran had called up to pass on an unhappy news. Sebastian and Kiran, both, were members of college handball team. They had represented the college in handball for three years. Among the team members, there was one person named Sushil. After college, Sebastian had not been in touch with Sushil at all. Sushil was a jolly, humorous guy and the star player of the team. He played excellent handball and was the centre-forward player of the team. Sebastian and Kiran were good friends with Sushil.

Kiran had called up to check if Sebastian have read that day's newspaper. To this, Sebastian confirmed in affirmative. Kiran then asked if he had seen the obituary column and Sebastian was silent. Kiran informed that the obituary column had Sushil's news. He had left them all for his heavenly abode a few days back and his prayer ceremony was due next day. Kiran said it came as a shocking news for him to read this in the newspaper. Sebastian fell silent. It was equally a shocker for him. Sebastian never expected to get such a message about a friend like Sushil. Kiran continued saying Sushil had not married and was all alone. He had set up an exhibition-cum-event management company and had been successfully running it for the last five years. Kiran had been in touch with him all along till last six months and now came this news, which had shaken him to the core. Kiran inquired if Sebastian would be willing to join him for the prayer session. Sebastian confirmed, as he felt deeply sorry for his friend.

Next evening, Sebastian reached the venue for the prayer session. He had to travel nearly one hour to reach the place. All along he was thinking about the time he had spent with Sushil and Kiran, the way they played handball together, the way they travelled together and the manner in which they strategized to play the matches. The intermediary rest they took in between and the bottle of water they shared to cool down their tired bodies. The memories seemed so fresh, that he felt as if it had all happened yesterday! Sushil's caring nature was commendable. He was a good friend and helpful to all.

On reaching the venue, Sebastian parked his car and then he called up Kiran on his mobile just to check if he had reached. Kiran was on his way and hence Sebastian waited outside the prayer hall for him to reach. Once Kiran arrived, Sebastian went forward and hugged his friend who he was meeting in person after nearly six years. Both exchanged pleasantries and then walked inside the hall where Sushil's peace prayer had been organised.

The hall was a room that could accommodate around 100 people. It was already occupied by nearly 30 of them. Seats were arranged in a row and well-spaced. In the front side of the hall, a podium was made and in the centre of the podium was a large photo of Sushil with a rose garland around it. The vibrant smile on Sushil's face reminded Sebastian of his old time friend and the good times they had spent together. In a low voice, Sebastian spoke to Kiran and

Kiran also shared the same feelings and emotions that he was going through then. The room was filled with the fragrance of camphor lamps kept across the room. There was complete silence. All were sinking in deep sorrow of having lost a friend at a young age of 35 years.

Suddenly, the vibe within the hall changed, as the event management team took charge. Cyril, the head of the event management team within Sushil's organisation, came on the podium and announced that Sushil had made a will and he was appropriately compelled to follow the will in its full spirit. Cyril also announced that he was feeling a bit strange, however he would have to go through what Sushil had mentioned in his will. There were three wishes he wanted to be fulfilled and Cyril read out that each of his wish will have to be fulfilled one at a time.

First wish: Each of the person present there for the prayer meet should introduce each one of them in person to the other and then go on to meet the next person; thereby, everyone should know each other.

All thirty of them looked at each other a bit bewildered. It was obviously a weird wish and it had nothing to do with a peace prayer. However, for their old friend who was no more, they started introducing each other. Initially it was a bit formal; however after few handshakes, Sebastian observed that the introduction meeting was taking a different turn.

Each of them started saying how they were associated with Sushil and the kind of memory they had about him. No more the introductory meeting was about themselves, but about Sushil and by the time the entire process was over, it was more than two hours and everyone knew more about Sushil, as those who had come there were associated with him at different stages of his life. Some during his college days, like Sebastian and Kiran. Some during his first year of his career, some in his last six years as an entrepreneur, some working with him, some were his clients and all had some beautiful memories to share about him at different contact levels and varying emotions that were attached with him. This made all of them withdraw in silence after the entire session was over. All sank into their seats with heavy heart thinking about their friend, who they have lost for ever.

Noticing that the first wish was fulfilled, Cyril then took charge and announced that, the second wish Sushil had was that each person now should come on the podium and share atleast one sentence about himself and his association with Sushil and one thing he/she got to know about Sushil after his/her interaction with the rest of them.

The silence in the room was again disturbed, as a lot of murmuring started. This second wish was also a bit weird. However, most of them consoled themselves with the thought that they felt the same even with the first wish, but the way that turned out, may be this wish also would work out some deep thoughts. So let's respect and thank the departed soul for having thought about such a unique way of accepting obituaries for himself.

Each one went on to express their thoughts. It was Sebastian's turn. Sebastian went on to say "Hi friends, I am Sebastian, working with a pharma company as Head of Marketing. Sushil and I were in the same college. This person here, Kiran also was with us. We all three were a part of college handball team. Sushil was such a kind person and such a good friend. Sad, our life took such turns that after college, I couldn't keep in touch with my friend. Alas, today while talking to all of you, I have realised the ups and downs that Sushil went through in his life, the way he struggled and never let these impact his positivism and kept going. The manner in which he decided to start his own organisation and became a source of revenue generator for some, I'm sure his life must have been inspirational. Wish he could have stayed more and become a source of inspiration for few more! Wish he would have been alive… Wish I could have kept in contact with my friend…. Wish we all could have been of help to him during the downside of his life ….Probably we would not have lost our friend. I pray, let his soul rest in peace."

With folded hands, Sebastian thanked everyone and came down from the podium. He was covering his face with his hands, trying to hide his emotions behind it. So were all of them who spoke about Sushil and prayed for his noble soul. Each of them were going through a disturbed moment, as if someone had shaken them by the roots and made them realise the importance of that one person in their respective lives.

After this, a feel of deep emotion with silence prevailed in the room and each of them were soaked in their own emotions of their association with Sushil.

Cyril was also sitting silently in one corner of the room. After letting a few moments pass in silence, Cyril came back on the podium and said, "Now we go to the last wish of Sushil" and saying this, he opened the envelope again, where the third wish was mentioned. Cyril, thus read it out: "I wished to party with my friends and hence after praying for me, the bar should be opened and dinner should be served to all attendees!"

Everyone was perplexed to hear this. One person got up and yelled at Cyril, "What the hell is going on? First the introduction, then a speech, now dinner with drinks!! Is this a prayer meet or a felicitation going on? Why did Sushil make such a will? Can you tell us why?"

Cyril, with a small smile on his face, said "For this, you will have to speak to Sushil."

The man got further wild and said, "Now you are talking like a stupid man. How can I ask Sushil, who is no more?"

Cyril then waved his hand to the screen behind and the screen was pulled down. A door opened and in walked Sushil!! Everyone was shocked to see him coming in. A person on the aisle seat on second last row saw him walking past, got up, caught hold of Sushil's collar from behind, turned him and slapped him hard. Sushil responded with a smile and hugged him. Few shouted un-parliamentary words and were about to leave the room, as they felt their time was taken for granted. But then they noticed that the doors were locked from outside, hence they couldn't leave.

Sushil reached the podium. One person in anger, threw his slipper at Sushil. Sushil caught it at the right moment and kept it down. All this time he had a smile on his face. He was wearing a white shirt and a white pant. Sebastian was silently observing his friend and his smile with vibrancy. Sushil ran his eyes through the assembled crowd and waved at each of them. His eyes had a special glare when he saw Sebastian and Kiran. He expressed in action that he shall catch up in specific with both of them later.

Cyril and his team of four members, suddenly became active, trying to calm and make everyone sit down. Few in anger were pouncing to get on the podium to hit Sushil. Two other employees of Sushil were protecting Sushil to prevent any such incident from happening.

Then, Sushil took control of the situation and spoke from the podium: "I faked my death!!. Yes, I faked it and celebrated it....the reason is all of you."

Everyone were looking at each other with a question mark on their face.

Sushil continued, "I have been living all alone for the last three years. Even though I had my work, my business and my good employees around me, I always had a vacuum in my life. I missed good friends. A good friend is someone with whom I could share my feelings, someone with whom I could talk to and express, someone who won't judge me but understand me, someone whose presence shall comfort me. I know for sure in this world everyone has few good friends, but we are so busy in our materialistic life that we never bother to take out time to spend those moments with our friend. Imagine what would have been Arjuna without Krishna, what would have been Duryodana without a Karna, what would have been Sudama without a Krishna, what would have been Vibhishana without Rama? We all need a good friend to stand by us in the hour of need. Today standing here, I can proudly say that I have a great circle of friends who cares for me. I have more than 30 friends who, just seeing an obituary column in the paper, decided to come for my prayer meeting. This is the biggest treasure I have created for myself."

He continued, "Your anger is fully justified and I apologise for what I have done. But, just rewind the time half hour back. Didn't you all wish that I should have still been alive, and, lo, here I am standing in front of you! Isn't it a moment of celebration than expressing anger? This is precisely what we are going through in our life. When someone is around, we suppress our feelings and never tell them how much we care about them. When that person is gone, the dam of sorrow breaks open and we suddenly start seeing and talking so much good about that person, instead of the routine back-biting we tend to do when the person is alive.. In the first wish, I gave you that opportunity to talk good/ bad about me. In a normal situation, all bad would have come out, but since you all believed that I am no more, all of you spoke good about me. What's the use of talking good about someone who is no more? Talk good when he is around, thereby wish good for the person and spread positivism across as well for self.

In the second wish, you were asked to speak about yourself and me and what you got to know about me. I was hearing all that you spoke, sitting in the next room. Probably, may be, first time you would have spoken less about yourself and more about me. The way each of you expressed about me, I was wondering, am I really so good? You all were fabulously good in expressing the way you all cared for me and how much you wished I was still with you. I remember one of my old time friend, whom I have not met for last six years, was mentioning how much he misses me now and wished he would have been in contact with me. This is what I was mentioning. When a person is around, we don't care for them. Please note, we all have an expiry date and once we are gone, your true friends will come and cry for you. But what's the use? You were not there when he really needed you. I need you all and this was the only way I could pull you all out together and bring you all to a common platform.

I am a lucky person to know who all shall cry when I shall die and I am happy that I have some real good friends who care for me and I love you all for having come here today. You all wished that I should have been alive and when you saw me, why this anger? This, my friends is the reality of life. If we look at this positively, you all should have embraced me with happiness that I am still around with all of you. Instead, few of you who wished me alive few minutes back got upset and wild with my sudden presence. This is because you suddenly moved from an inclusive space that you created for me in my absence to an exclusive space of yours after seeing me. But I know, deep in your heart you still care for me, else you wouldn't have come today.

You all have prayed for my peace and that has increased my life. Today, standing here I can happily and proudly say, the biggest treasure I have is you all and I know now who I can contact when I need to speak to someone. It is you, my loving friends. Thanks so much for making this day for me.

I hope, my act must have been an eye-opener and a message to all of you that life should be with inclusivity that has people outside your close family borders artificially created by each one of us. We are social animals and we need to be socially accepted. You have the power to be accepted, as well as accept others. Go live life to the fullest.

The day when I stand in front of my God, and if he asks me, I sent you to live, tell me how was your experience of heaven? I would be proud enough to say, thank you my Lord, the heaven was beautiful with my friends always with me!!

Now, as a thanksgiving to my loving friends, I move on to my third wish in life in good spirit. Let's party together and celebrate the life of togetherness. God bless all."

Sushil got down from the podium and went on to embrace each person. Everyone in the room was rooted and hence couldn't move after having experienced what they have gone through and the message given by their friend. After hugging their friend, they sat back to their seat in deep thoughts. Cyril and his friends had a difficult time convincing all to move to the next room where dinner and music with DJ was organised.

That night everyone danced and celebrated like there was no yesterday and there will be no tomorrow.

A meaningful life is not being rich, being popular, being highly educated or being perfect. It is all about being real, BEING HUMBLE, being able to share ourselves and touch the lives of others, positively.

God bless all!!!

ABOUT THE AUTHOR

Ajit Nair is Mumbai-based, qualified Chartered Accountant. Ajit has worked in various functions in reputed companies over the last twenty five years.

During his tenure in the industry, Ajit had opportunities to experience various situations and deal with interesting people - each of who were appealing in their own way and had unique stories to share. This book is a genuine effort by Ajit to give life to those select stories that have had a positive impact on him, so as to share the positivity with his readers.

This book is his attempt to play a squirrel's role in the gigantic task of letting people know how being humble helps in EMBRACING EPIPHANY MOMENT and overcoming all situations

This is Ajit's second book.

His debut literary effort was a book called "KHUSHI - Short Inspirational Stories For Kids". This book was to help parents share beautiful, inspirational and motivating short stories with their kids, to help inculcate positive thinking in them. It also aimed towards creating a strong bonding between the parents and children away from the celluloid screens. All proceeds to the author from the sale of this book were diverted to a NGO named Khushi, that supports children with Autism.